THE CHRISTIAN IMAGINATION

THOMAS C. PETERS

THE
CHRISTIAN
IMAGINATION

G. K. Chesterton on the Arts

IGNATIUS PRESS   SAN FRANCISCO

Cover art by Christopher J. Pelicano
Cover design by Roxanne Mei Lum

© 2000 Ignatius Press, San Francisco
All rights reserved
ISBN 0–89870–757–9
Library of Congress catalogue number 99–73017
Printed in the United States of America ⊗

To the Mermaid

CONTENTS

PREFACE

"I wonder at not wondering." Thus ends a short poem[1] by G. K. Chesterton, expressing perhaps better than any other of his words the essence of this great Christian writer and artist. For Chesterton was a man who believed passionately that we need to imagine and to wonder; that we need surprise and adventure; that we need laughter and play; that we truly need art, poetry, drama, and songs. To Chesterton these needs are not simply a matter of frivolity or even of psychological well-being; they reach into the very core of what it means to live consistently with the intention of the Creator. For the Christian they reach into the very purpose of existence and faith: "to glorify God and to enjoy him forever".[2] Chesterton wondered at not wondering; in other words, he found it astonishing—and troubling—that so many of us let our imaginations die and cease to wonder.

The guiding theme of this study is the imagination, and more specifically the Christian imagination according to G. K. Chesterton. Particularly in his masterpiece *Orthodoxy*, Chesterton insisted that we are created to live our lives as an adventure[3] and that such things as art and wonder and play lie

---

[1] G. K. Chesterton, "The Mystery", in *The Works of G. K. Chesterton* (Hertfordshire, Eng.: Wordsworth Editions, 1995), 51–52.

[2] "The Shorter Catechism", article 7.001 in *The Book of Confessions* (Louisville, Ky.: Presbyterian Church-USA, 1983).

[3] G. K. Chesterton, *Orthodoxy*, "Authority and the Adventurer" in *The Collected Works of G. K. Chesterton*, vol. 1 (San Francisco: Ignatius Press, 1986), 346–66.

at the very core of the Christian faith rightly understood. Indeed, in his *Autobiography* he wrote:

> [B]ut I for one have never left off playing, and I wish there were more time to play. I wish we did not have to fritter away on frivolous things, like lectures and literature, the time we might have given to serious, solid and constructive work like cutting out cardboard figures and pasting coloured tinsel upon them.[4]

Chesterton asserted that there is much more to Christian faith than intellectual assent and moral conformity to the creeds and doctrines. Faith, in fact, embraces imagination.

There is much here concerning the arts in all of their genres, including the visual and performing arts, literature and poetry—and certainly including popular songs. It is significant that in *The Everlasting Man* Chesterton placed so much importance on the imaginative arts in defining our humanness.[5] On the one hand, our creative arts demonstrate our qualitative difference from the other animal species; on the other hand, our creative arts reflect in a small way the fact that we are fashioned in the image of the greatest Creator of all. To be human, said Chesterton, is to be imaginative and creative, and when we create we are doing what God endowed and intended us to do.

Here we will examine this remarkable man, G. K. Chesterton, as artist and Christian, paying particular attention to his insights into imaginative expression. First we will imbibe a sampling of Chesterton's own work as a songwriter, a poet, a storyteller, a dramatist, an essayist, and an illustrator. Next we will look at his thoughts on the nature of the Christian

[4] G. K. Chesterton, *Autobiography*, The Collected Works of G. K. Chesterton, vol. 16 (San Francisco: Ignatius Press, 1988), 50.

[5] G. K. Chesterton, *The Everlasting Man*, in *The Collected Works of G. K. Chesterton*, vol. 2 (San Francisco: Ignatius Press, 1986), 161–66.

imagination and the forces that work to oppose and destroy its vitality. We will explore further his specific comments concerning the various manifestations of the imagination, especially regarding written expression, the performing arts, and the visual arts. Consistent with Chesterton's belief that the true Christian enjoys a very special relationship with the Author of creativity, we will conclude with an outline of Chesterton's theology of imagination. And finally, we will visit briefly the life and times of this topsy-turvy giant, G. K. Chesterton.

To study G. K. Chesterton is to enter a world where imagination takes center stage. Chesterton himself was among the most creative of the great Christian writers, and he held a profound belief in the potential holiness of the arts as "the wild whisper of something originally wise".[6] It is for this reason, Chesterton believed, that the imagination is to be treasured and nurtured, as it replicates that Divine Creativity to which we owe our hopes, our faith, our joys, our loves, and our very lives.

[6] *Orthodoxy*, 283.

Chapter One

A G. K. Chesterton Palette

Gilbert Keith Chesterton is widely recognized as a brilliant and entertaining Christian apologist and a fierce defender of the faith. The legendary wit and wisdom of G. K. Chesterton have delighted generations of his readers for nearly a century, and few have not at one time or another heard the familiar preface, "As G. K. Chesterton once said...". What is perhaps less well known about Chesterton is his lifelong love relationship with the arts. Though he claimed mastery in none of the arts, Chesterton was in fact a respectable writer of songs, poetry, drama, essays, short stories, and novels, as well as an accomplished illustrator and cartoonist.

There are two reasons why the name G. K. Chesterton is sure to arise in any contemplation on the Christian imagination and the arts. First is the fact that G. K. was himself an artist of remarkable abilities and amazing breadth. Second is the prodigious outpouring of commentary on the arts that appears throughout the more than ninety books he wrote during his lifetime. Our intention here is to sample briefly a few specimens of Chesterton's various talents before proceeding into a more detailed exploration of his ideas on imagination and the arts.

Chesterton loved the arts because he was an incurable Romantic as well as a frolicsome child of the great Creator. His

works were part of a broader movement in reaction and opposition to the mechanistic and dehumanizing aspects of the
scientism[1] and commercial industrialism of the nineteenth
and twentieth centuries. Because of his orthodox and revolutionary faith, Chesterton stands as a major figure among
such other Christian Romantics as George MacDonald,
J. R. R. Tolkien, Owen Barfield, Dorothy Sayers, and C. S.
Lewis. All of these writers sought to establish the faithful
response to the cult of scientism—an outgrowth of the materialist Enlightenment world view—by asserting once again
the unique, creative, and spiritual aspects of the human being.

While all of the Christian Romantics were naturally drawn
to creative expression, few were so prolific or so broadly tal-
ented as G. K. Chesterton. Though G. K. always remained
humble with regard to his talents, he nevertheless produced
a truly amazing array of first-rate work in several genres. Here
we shall seize the rare pleasure of dabbling on the colorful
palette of G. K. Chesterton's artistic genius, as we look in
turn at brief samplings from his songs, his poetry, his stories,
his plays, his essays, and his illustrations.

Probably the most famous of Chesterton's songs is his
Christmas carol that begins like this:

> The Christ-child lay on Mary's lap,
>   His hair was like a light
> (O weary, weary were the world
>   But here is all aright.)[2]

This song is full of tenderness and awe for the Christ child
and his significance to human history. It is important to note
here at the onset that Chesterton was a man whose Christian

[1] Michael Aeschliman, *The Restitution of Man: C. S. Lewis and the Case against
Scientism* (Grand Rapids, Mich.: W. B. Eerdmans, 1983), 35.
[2] *The Collected Works of G. K. Chesterton*, vol. 10, pt. 1 (San Francisco: Ignatius Press, 1994), 126.

faith permeated his art. Having converted to Christianity as an adult for his own well-considered reasons, G. K. lived his life with the grateful and glorious energy of a man who truly believed that he had been saved from sure destruction. As there was nothing apologetic in his apologetics, neither was there any reticence or "tasteful subtlety" to dim the glow of his faith in his writings and drawings.

Most of his songs, however, are what G. K. liked to call "drinking-songs", uproarious communal songs intended for the purposes of fun and comradeship. Many of these songs can be found in context in Chesterton's novels—particularly in *The Flying Inn*.[3] Others can be found among his poetry collections and in his more light-hearted books, like *Greybeards at Play*.[4]

A great example illustrating Chesterton's penchant for mixing apparent nonsense with profound meaning is his "The Song of Quoodle", which is a song ostensibly written by a dog named Quoodle. Here the author uses the unique point of view of a dog to comment upon some of the obvious failings of human beings. The song begins:

> They haven't got no noses,
> The fallen sons of Eve,
> Even the smell of roses
> Is not what they supposes,
> But more than mind discloses,
> And more than men believe.[5]

The song then goes on to express the dog's dismay at the poverty of human olfactory perception, and especially at the great wonders of which humans are unaware. For example:

[3] G. K. Chesterton, *The Flying Inn* (London: Methuen and Company, 1919).

[4] G. K. Chesterton, *Greybeards at Play* (London: Elek, 1974).

[5] *The Collected Works of G. K. Chesterton*, vol. 10, pt. 1 (San Francisco: Ignatius Press, 1994), 477.

The smell of dew and thunder,
The old bones buried under,
Are things in which they blunder.[6]

This song is a marvelous opportunity to join imaginatively
with the dogs for an insiders' joke about those "noseless"
human creatures.

After having sung and laughed along, however, one comes
to realize that Chesterton is up to much more than merely
using the canine perspective to satirize human perception.
As it turns out, this playful song reaches into the depths of its
author's philosophy and theology, as Quoodle's words contain Chesterton's critique of scientism—a popular belief hold-
ing that reality consists only in what we can perceive with
our senses.[7] Thus, in this one, short song G. K. not only
questions the adequacy of human perception but also de-
bunks the idea of believing only what one can see—or, in
this case, smell.

Surely, the words "more than mind discloses/And more than
men believe" are an ingenious way of showing the folly of
founding one's beliefs solely upon one's perceptions. Even the
dog Quoodle is baffled at the realities that humans do not perceive, and here the animal reflects Chesterton's perennial campaign to awaken his readers to the wonders of everyday life.
And of course as a Christian, G. K. takes the argument a step
farther in recognizing the hidden reality of the spiritual realm
and of the miracles that we have taught ourselves not to notice. "The Song of Quoodle", then, is a playful wake-up call
to people who are missing what is most important in life because they apparently "haven't got no noses".

Besides Chesterton's songs both serious and playful, there
is his poetry. His poems fill the spectrum from nonsense

6. Ibid.
7. *Restitution of Man*, 35.

rhymes through social satire to epic verse. Of playful nonsense there is plenty. One example derives from G. K.'s hope-
less failure to understand mathematics at school. In these
excerpts from a rhyme called "True Sympathy", he speaks
of himself and his mathematics teacher:

> The point was without magnitude;
>   I knew without regret
> Our minds were moving parallel
>   Because they never met. . . .
>
> That he should think I thought he thought
>   That X was ABC
> Was far, far happier for him
>   And possibly for me. . . .
>
> And Mathematics merged and met
>   Its Higher Unity,
> Where five and two and twelve and four
>   They all were One to me.[8]

In reading Chesterton's playful poetry, however, one must
always keep watching for a more serious intent. Much of his
apparent tomfoolery turns out to have a biting edge. For
example, one of his pet peeves was the showy humanitarian
who actually cared very little for real individual people. In a
poem called "The World State", G. K. wrote facetiously:

> Oh, how I love Humanity,
>   With love so pure and pringlish,
> And how I hate the horrid French,
>   Who never will be English!

And so the poem goes with sarcastic gaiety into the final
stanza:

[8] *Greybeards at Play*, 88.

> The villas and the chapels where
> I learned with little labour
> The way to love my fellow-man
> And hate my next-door neighbour.[9]

More times than not, the harmless Chestertonian rhyme proves to contain a deeper meaning that emerges amid the laughter.

Reading Chesterton's poetry can be a delightful experience indeed, and in time one begins to fathom the depths of the man's creative genius. In a remarkable poem called "Variations on an Air: Composed on Having to Appear in a Pageant as Old King Cole", G. K. displays the breadth of his talent by writing consecutive stanzas in the poetic styles of Tennyson, Yeats, Browning, Whitman, and Swinburne, respectively. The result is both comedic and astounding. As we know, the traditional rhyme goes:

> Old King Cole was a merry old soul,
> And a merry old soul was he;
> He called for his pipe,
> He called for his bowl,
> And he called for his fiddlers three.

Now, here is a small sample of Chesterton's rendition in the style of Walt Whitman:

> The crown cannot hide you from me;
> Musty old feudal-heraldic trappings
>   cannot hide you from me....
> I see you are inhaling tobacco,
>   puffing, smoking, spitting
> (I do not object to your spitting),

---

[9] *Collected Works*, vol. 10, pt. 1, 528.

> You prophetic of American largeness,
> You anticipating the broad masculine
> manners of these States.[10]

Though Whitman was one of Chesterton's favorite poets, G. K. was not averse to having some fun with the Whitman style. But amusement grows to amazement as Chesterton captures the style of each poet in his turn.

Certainly, not all of Chesterton's poems are playful. There are numerous poems about such subjects as heroism, love of one's country, and faith in God, revealing an author who with all seriousness is expressing his thoughts to the reading world. There is, for example, a poem called "The Donkey", wherein the homely beast laments its lowly status as a "walking parody" among the creatures. And yet, the final lines tell a different story:

> Starve, scourge, deride me; I am dumb,
> I keep my secret still.

> Fools! For I also had my hour,
> One far fierce hour and sweet:
> There was a shout about my ears,
> And palms before my feet.[11]

Perhaps for the first time the reader ponders the Savior's choice of mount for his triumphal ride into Jerusalem, and the discerning reader is reminded once more of the Christian paradox of the greatest and the least.

Ignoring the fact that the literary world had relegated epic poetry as a thing of the past, G. K. was apt to use this form whenever he was greatly moved in speaking of heroism, honor,

---

[10] *The Works of G. K. Chesterton* (Hertfordshire, Eng.: Wordsworth Editions, 1995), 38.
[11] *Collected Works*, vol. 10, pt. 1, 134.

courage, perseverance, and other disappearing virtues. One
such epic poem is "Lepanto", in which Chesterton tells the
story of Austria's Don John mounting a crusade against the
Turks to free the captives held in Spain. Here the author
contrasts the indolence of the various Christian monarchs
with the heroic action of Don John. For example:

> The cold queen of England is looking in the glass;
> The shadow of the Valois is yawning at the Mass;
> From evening isles fantastical rings faint
>   the Spanish gun,
> And the Lord upon the Golden Horn
>   is laughing in the sun.[12]

And so, while Christendom sleeps and the Turkish tyrant
laughs at its imminent demise, the courageous Don John alone
rushes to its defense. Here is heroic epic verse as one seldom
sees it in poetry today:

Dim drums throbbing, in the hills half heard,
Where only on a nameless throne a crownless prince
    has stirred,
Where, risen from a doubtful seat and half-attainted
    stall,
The last knight of Europe takes weapons from the wall,
The last and lingering troubadour
    to whom the bird has sung,
That once went southward singing when all the world
    was young.
In that enormous silence, tiny and unafraid,
Comes up along a winding road the noise of the
    Crusade.[13]

[12] Ibid., 548.
[13] Ibid., 549.

Among Chesterton's many strong opinions was the assertion that the things of the past—whether they be notions of heroism or accepted forms of poetry—are often as valid today as when they enjoyed their greatest popularity. Unreflecting "presentism" in life and art is a habit that Chesterton never tired of denouncing.

G. K. Chesterton's greatest initial success, however, came from his mastery as a teller of stories. His personal favorite genre was the kind of short story commonly called the murder mystery, and it was through his wildly popular Father Brown mysteries that he first gained fame in Europe and North America. The Father Brown collections are still in print and selling briskly to this very day.

The true genius of the Father Brown mysteries is that they intrigue and entertain, while at the same time they reflect the author's perspective on life as derived from his Christian faith. Put most simply, Chesterton strongly believed that human behavior can be understood much better through the window of the soul than through the strictly rational-empirical methods of positive science. Consequently, in the stories it is a plain, unsophisticated priest who unravels the mysteries that the experts cannot solve.

As in so many of the classic, great detective stories, there is always that pivotal moment when the protagonist thrills the reader with a sudden flash of revelation. A typical Chestertonian flash is captured in the excellent story "The Hammer of God":

> Father Brown had fixed his eyes on the speaker so long and steadily as to prove that his large grey, ox-like eyes were not quite so insignificant as the rest of his face. When silence had fallen he said with marked respect: "Mr. Bohun, yours is the only theory yet propounded which holds water every way and is essentially unassailable. I think, therefore, that you

deserve to be told, on my positive knowledge, that it is not the true one." [14]

Apparently no man of great intellect like Sherlock Holmes or Lord Peter Wimsey, the pedestrian priest nevertheless reveals the murderer. How does he do it? The priest sees beyond the obvious conclusions from the stark facts and logic; as a religious man he is willing to open his mind to possibilities to which the others turn a blind, disbelieving eye. Watching how Chesterton draws this golden thematic thread through his mysteries is one of the signal pleasures to be found in reading the Father Brown stories.

G. K. Chesterton was also author of several novels. Though his novels in general are not of the quality to bring literary critical acclaim, many of them are a great pleasure to read nevertheless. In his novels G. K. tends to create characters who clearly represent extant ideas and then to put them into conflict as the plot of the story. Even granting that the results are sometimes artistically clumsy, Chesterton's novels are never uninteresting.

Of the many fascinating episodes from which to choose among Chesterton's novels, one from *The Poet and the Lunatics* will serve as a good example. Here, poet and painter Gabriel Gale has been tricked by two unscrupulous physicians who intend to commit him to an asylum for madness. Speaking of Gale, Chesterton writes:

> But it was characteristic of him that even when he was practically hopeless, he liked being logically triumphant; he liked turning the tables on his critics even when, so to speak, they were as abstract as multiplication tables.
>
> "Why, my learned friends," he went on contemptuously, "do you really suppose that you are any fitter to write a report on my mind than I am on yours? You can't see any

[14] G. K. Chesterton, *Father Brown Crime Stories* (New York: Avenal Books, 1990), 248–49.

further into me than I can into you. Not half so far. Didn't you know a portrait painter has to value people at sight as much as a doctor? And I do it better than you; I have a knack that way.... I know what is at the back of your mind, Doctor Simeon Wolfe; and it's a chaos of exceptions with no rule. You could find anything abnormal, because you have no normal. You could find anybody mad...." [15]

Aside from the provocative idea of art challenging psychology, this passage serves as a great example of Chesterton's use of his characters to argue his concepts. Like much of his writing—both fiction and nonfiction—his novels often explore the interplay of art, madness, philosophy, and faith.

Among Chesterton's artistic talents, drama was not his most successful, but he did enjoy immensely his rare forays as a playwright. There were several plays from G. K.'s pen, the first of which was the play called *Magic*. Here the author uses the antics of a hired conjurer to pit materialist philosophy against supernaturalism. At one point in the play, the subject of miracles arises, as one of the skeptical characters seeks to disprove the supernatural on the basis of having seen miracles exposed as shams. Another character responds with classic Chestertonian logic. He says:

Why should sham miracles prove to us that real Saints and Prophets never lived? There may be sham magic and real magic also.... There may be theatrical fairies precisely because there are real fairies. You do not abolish the Bank of England by pointing to a forged bank-note. [16]

It is a fascinating play, in which Chesterton explores the relationships among materialism, supernaturalism, madness, and sanity.

[15] G. K. Chesterton, *The Poet and the Lunatics* (London: Cassell and Company, 1929), 259.
[16] G. K. Chesterton, *Magic* in *The Collected Works of G. K. Chesterton*, vol. 11 (San Francisco: Ignatius Press, 1989), 125.

Among the most entertaining and rewarding of Chesterton's several manifestations of artistic genius are his essays. These marvelous little masterpieces appeared in the London newspapers and magazines, constituting the labor by which GKC managed to pay his bills and support his household. Even at the very height of his fame and creative productivity, Chesterton always insisted that he was "merely a journalist" and nothing more.

His essays, however, rise far above the level of journalism found in the papers even by the superior standards of his day, and many have been gathered into delightful collections with names like *All Things Considered*[17] and *Tremendous Trifles*[18] and *All Is Grist*.[19] His topics are as varied as his imagination is rich, but there is always that surprising Chestertonian wit and the strong undercurrent that is his Christian faith.

As a sample of Chesterton's style in his essays, consider the following offhand remark on the fantasies of Lewis Carroll, author of *Alice in Wonderland*. In an essay called "A Defense of Nonsense", G. K. writes:

> His Wonderland is a country populated by insane mathematicians. We feel the whole is an escape into a world of masquerade; we feel that if we could pierce their disguises, we might discover that Humpty Dumpty and the March Hare were Professors and Doctors of Divinity enjoying a mental holiday.[20]

But of course, one must read the entire essay in order to enjoy the full impact of Chesterton's use of logic and language.

---

[17] G. K. Chesterton, *All Things Considered* (London: Methuen and Company, 1915).

[18] G. K. Chesterton, *Tremendous Trifles* (New York: Dodd, Mead and Company, 1910).

[19] G. K. Chesterton, *All Is Grist* (New York: Books for Libraries Press, 1967).

[20] G. K. Chesterton, *The Defendant* (London: J. M. Dent and Sons, 1907), 66.

In another sample, from an essay called "A Healthy Madness", Chesterton's own imagination nearly steals the show. In the midst of a discussion of pantomime, he writes:

> To the quietest human being, seated in the quietest house, there will sometimes come a sudden and unmeaning hunger for the possibilities or impossibilities of things; he will abruptly wonder whether the teapot may not suddenly begin to pour out honey or sea-water, the clock to point to all hours of the day at once, the candle to burn green or crimson, the door to open upon a lake or a potato-field instead of a London street.[21]

If the thought of reading essays brings images of somnolent poring over dry exposition, a bracing dose of Chesterton's essays should erase that notion forever.

Finally, G. K. Chesterton loved to draw. During his school days he spent much of his time dawdling and doodling on his papers, while neglecting his proper studies to the point of reaching the bottom of his class. Though he also failed to thrive in his subsequent venture to an art school, G. K. nevertheless continued his habit of sketching and cartooning over his entire life. He illustrated some of his own books, and particularly in *Greybeards at Play* his sketches add mightily to the fun of its reading. He also illustrated other authors' books, including many of the novels of his friend Hilaire Belloc. Throughout his career as a journalist, Chesterton's cartoons appeared in various London newspapers and later more frequently in his own *G. K.'s Weekly* journal. Here is a sample cartoon that accompanied Chesterton's poem "The Oneness of the Philosopher with Nature" as found in the collection *Greybeards at Play*.[22]

This cartoon is typical of Chesterton's style of illustration, as it combines an engaging simplicity and playfulness with a

---

[21] Ibid., 125.
[22] *Greybeards at Play*, 16.

satiric meaning. In this drawing the overly confident philosopher lies back and balances a star on the tip of his nose.

Here we have sampled the varied and fascinating fruits of
Chesterton's genius as a prelude to a more substantive study
of his thoughts on imagination. Though Chesterton never
claimed any kind of scholarly expertise on imagination, the
arts, or anything else for that matter, it will become increas-
ingly clear that he had pondered these matters a great deal
and had applied his formidable insight to their many aspects.
It is helpful to know that this man who so freely spoke his
thoughts and opinions drew from the rich soil of his own
experiences in the arts, rather than from the usual superficial
survey of experts quoting experts. Among Chesterton's ideas
the alert reader will no doubt find something to deplore,
possibly more to praise, but at any rate a great deal to enjoy

along the way. For this man who enjoyed debating George Bernard Shaw and Clarence Darrow was not looking for settled agreement; he was looking for intelligent discourse in pursuit of the truth. For those hearty and imaginative souls who can enjoy the art of a good controversy, the table is set and the meal is now served.

Chapter Two

The Christian Imagination

Throughout his many and varied writings, G. K. Chesterton had much to say concerning imagination and the arts. He was not one, however, to bloat himself with the illusion that he spoke as a learned expert on the topic. Though G. K. was himself a remarkably imaginative and creative artist, he nevertheless possessed the sense to recognize the extreme difficulties involved in defining exactly what the imagination is. In his discussions of the arts, Chesterton very often used the words *poet* and *poetic* when he obviously meant to include the broader ideas of the imaginative, or of the artist and the artistic. Thus, when he wrote of the mysterious life of the imagination, he meant certainly to include the arts in general. Regarding imaginative artists he wrote:

> They live by that mysterious life of the imagination, which is something much more terrible than an anarchy. For it has laws of its own which man has never been able to turn into a code. But anyone who understands poetry knows when poetry has fulfilled those laws; as certainly as a mathematician knows when a mathematical calculation is correct. Only, the mathematician can explain, more or less, why the answer is exactly right; and the lover of poetry can never explain why the word or the image is exactly right.... The poet is riding the air on the imagination alone; and his Pegasus

has wings and no feet. But almost all that has been attempted, in the way of analyzing those imaginative laws, has
been done by some metaphysician, who has feet and no
wings.[1]

No one, observed Chesterton, has really satisfactorily ana-
lyzed the laws of imagination, and G. K. made no pretensions as to having even attempted to do so himself.

Having thus excused himself for lack of a precise
definition—that is, for not having done the impossible—
Chesterton then proceeded nevertheless to say a great many
insightful and fascinating things about human imagination,
creativity, and the arts. As a poet and songwriter, a storyteller and novelist, an essayist, a dramatist, and an illustrator,
G. K. brought a respectable reservoir of practical experience
into his observations. As a philosopher and a Christian, he
was able to take the larger view in discussing the meanings
and significance of what he saw and experienced in the world
around him. One of the most fundamental issues he tackled
was the role of imagination in the very nature of the human
being.

Flying in the face of the evolutionary theory that was so
very popular at the dawn of the twentieth century, G. K.
Chesterton laid a great deal of stress on the fact that human
beings are a prodigy and a mystery among the animals. The
difference, he insisted, between humans and even their clos-
est "relatives" is so qualitatively significant as to render the
idea of a gradual and accidental development unlikely to the
point of the preposterous. The human animal does not simply possess higher intelligence, Chesterton observed, but humans display a kind of consciousness completely different
from that of other creatures.

[1] G. K. Chesterton, *As I Was Saying* (New York: Books for Libraries Press, 1966), 87–88.

The human sciences have been unable to discern this qualitative difference in humanity, Chesterton argued, because they have tried to observe the human creature narrowly, as if through a microscope. In turning the limited eye of the natural sciences toward humanity itself, the sciences have made some wonderful discoveries—for example, in the field of medicine—but they have unfortunately blinded themselves to the larger and more important picture. G. K. put it this way:

> Looked at thus microscopically, man may be made to appear as commonplace and mechanical as a larva or an amoeba; but looked at simply and suddenly, looked at in its whole bulk and proportion, the position of man in nature is a monstrous and miraculous thing. It is like seeing a hundred toadstools an inch high and another toadstool forty feet high.[2]

Chesterton was ever fond of pointing out the irony in hearing the only animal even capable of pondering the meaning of its existence trying to insist that it is really just like the other creatures, only a little more so.

For Chesterton the central issue here was human imagination and creativity, and the pivotal data were the arts. In *The Everlasting Man* he pointed out that there is no record of any other animal—besides the human—dabbling in even the most primitive of arts. Of course being of the imaginative sort himself, Chesterton could not resist a playful interlude with the idea:

> An entertaining fantasia might be made in which elephants built in elephantine architecture, with towers and turrets like tusks and trunks, cities beyond the scale of any colossus. A peasant fable might be conceived in which a cow developed a costume, and put on four boots and two pair of trousers.

[2] G. K. Chesterton, *Lunacy and Letters* (New York: Sheed and Ward, 1958), 36.

> We could imagine a Supermonkey more marvelous than any
> Superman, a quadrumanous creature carving and painting
> with his hands and cooking and carpentering with his feet.[3]

Surely it is fun to fantasize as such, Chesterton reasoned,
"but anyone facing what did happen must face an exception
and a prodigy".[4] The broad and honest view of animal and
human life makes it abundantly clear that human imagination is a thing not even approximated in the other species.
   Developing this point even more forcefully, GKC added:

> It is the simple truth that man does differ from the brutes in
> kind and not in degree; and the proof of it is here; that it
> sounds like a truism to say that the most primitive man drew
> a picture of a monkey and it sounds like a joke to say that the
> most intelligent monkey drew a picture of a man. Some-
> thing of division and disproportion has appeared; and it is
> unique. Art is the signature of man.[5]

Chesterton's point was that if one takes an unbiased look at
the available facts in the matter, one must admit that there
are no animals—except for humans—that display even the
crudest propensity for artistic expression. From this he concluded, "This creature was truly different from all other creatures; because he was a creator as well as a creature."[6]
   As the primary expression of human imagination, the arts
therefore assumed a role of utmost importance in Chesterton's views on humanity. It is no exaggeration to say that he
considered the arts to reflect the very essence of human nature as endowed by God the Creator. Here is what G.K.
meant when he wrote, "I cannot feel myself that art has any

[3] G.K. Chesterton, *The Everlasting Man*, in *The Collected Works of G.K. Chesterton*, vol. 2 (San Francisco: Ignatius Press, 1986), 151.
   [4] Ibid.
   [5] Ibid., 166.
   [6] Ibid., 167.

dignity higher than the indwelling and divine dignity of human nature." [7] In another context he referred to "using our own imagination: that is, our own inside knowledge of humankind". [8] Thus, it is our imagination and our arts that define us as human. Conversely, if we allow ourselves to lose our imagination and we cease to practice our arts, we thereby become something inhuman or at least less than fully human.

We are imaginative and creative creatures, said Chesterton, because we are made in the image of the great Creator of all. Yes, in our fallen state we have lost a major portion of our original endowment, yet we retain a portion of it as well. In his *Lunacy and Letters*, G. K. explained:

> Lost somewhere in the enormous plains of time, there wanders a dwarf who is the image of God, who has produced on a yet more dwarfish scale an image of creation. The pigmy picture of God we call Man; the pigmy picture of creation we call Art. It is an undervaluing of the function of man to say that he only expresses his own personality.... His business (as something secondary but divine) is to make the world over again, and that is the meaning of all portraits and public buildings. [9]

There is much to digest here. Not only did Chesterton invoke the "image of God" as the source of human creativity, but in a sense he "baptized" the arts as at least one of our divine purposes.

In direct contradiction to the extant anthropological and psychological theories of the arts as expressions of the human mind, Chesterton suggested that the arts—faithfully and rightly practiced—derive from the divine endowment of human nature itself. The implications of this thought are

---

[7] G. K. Chesterton, *Varied Types* (New York: Dodd, Mead and Company, 1903), 256.

[8] G. K. Chesterton, *Generally Speaking* (New York: Dodd, Mead and Company, 1929), 120.

[9] *Lunacy and Letters*, 90.

tremendous, and the Christian artist who understands this
connection cannot help but fear and tremble at the gravity
of it and yet celebrate and exult in the glory of it. If Jesus
Christ is truly the God of creation, then the Christian imagination is nothing less than a direct connection to the very
Source of creation itself. As Chesterton pointed out, we are
like pigmies creating our pigmy arts, but in doing so we are
certainly imitating the Creator of all arts. To the extent that
a Christian can enter into the mind of God, to that extent
can his art fulfill that divine purpose of creation.

In his book *The Glass Walking-Stick*, G. K. wrote: "What
is wanted is the truly godlike imagination which makes all
things new, because all things have been new. That would
really be something like a new power of the mind." [10] Here
Chesterton came to the heart of Christian imagination, speaking of a new power of the mind. He was speaking of nothing
less than transcending the ordinary intellect and tapping into
that divine energy which makes the world new again and
again. This theme of making new what appears to be old
runs like a thread through the poetry, fiction, and nonfiction
writings of G. K. Chesterton.

In looking at the Christian imagination as expressive of
the Creator's attributes, Chesterton returned to the popular
anthropological wisdom on the art of the prehistoric cave-
dwellers. Particularly in his *The Everlasting Man*, G. K. had
great fun in delivering those well-deserved jabs at the many
officious speculations offered under the name of scientific
fact. Indeed, a review of the famous early studies reveals a
rather amusing sense of self-confidence based on the most
fragile skeletons of evidence, as study after study comes to
the same, predictable conclusions about the psychology of

---

[10] G. K. Chesterton, *The Glass Walking-Stick* (London: Methuen and Company, 1955), 166.

primitive arts and religions. Pointing out that one man's speculations are as valid as another's, Chesterton produced his own theory of cave art:

> The common sense of a child could confine itself to learning from the facts what the facts have to teach; and the pictures in the cave are very nearly all the facts there are. So far as the evidence goes, the child would be justified in assuming that a man had represented animals with rock and red ochre for the same reason as he himself was in the habit of trying to represent animals with charcoal and red chalk. The man had drawn a stag just as the child had drawn a horse; because it was fun.[11]

What a surprising hypothesis, and yet, why not? There is certainly no evidence to disprove it. Why should the idea of cave-dwellers drawing for fun seem any more preposterous than that of their drawing for some solemn purposes of mysterious superstitious significance? The only answer appears to be that a doctor of philosophy suggested the latter, while a frivolous journalist suggested the former.

The point, however, is far from frivolous. Besides his entirely justifiable rejection of the ostensibly "scientific" explanations of primitive humans and their superstitions, Chesterton's argument directs our attention to an essential element of the divine imagination: fun. In short, the Creator loves fun, and there is evidence of this everywhere, for those with eyes to see. Consider, for example, the hippopotamus, the sea-horse, and the platypus. These and a thousand other examples obviously reveal, not the accidental effects of a struggle for survival, but a conscious Creator with a taste for beauty and a sense of humor.

For Chesterton, an indispensable aspect of the divine imagination is the inclusion of fun. Play, laughter, joy, and mirth

[11] *Everlasting Man*, 163–64.

are necessary not only for good art but for human well-being in all its dimensions. G. K. once said that "in anything that does cover the whole of your life—in your philosophy and your religion—you must have mirth. If you do not have mirth you will certainly have madness." [12] If Chesterton was correct in these surmises, then the Christian imagination ought to be "like a fountain of living water" springing joyously from its divine source.

G. K. was fond of quoting Jesus' words, "Truly I say to you, whoever does not receive the kingdom of God like a child shall not enter it at all", [13] for Chesterton truly believed that in children can be found the unspoiled remnants of divinity. It is natural, then, that Chesterton would return to the child in his attempts to understand imagination. In this regard he wrote:

> There is something mysterious and perhaps more than mortal about the power and call of imagination. I do not think this early experience has been quite rightly understood, even by those modern writers who have written the most charming and fanciful studies of childhood. [14]

For Chesterton the key to imagination lay in the eyes of a child, and it was to his own childhood thoughts that he tried to return in his quest to understand. "What was wonderful about childhood", he wrote, "is that anything in it was a wonder. It was not merely a world full of miracles; it was a miraculous world ... like a hundred windows opened on all sides of the head." [15]

---

[12] *Lunacy and Letters*, 97.

[13] Luke 18:17.

[14] G. K. Chesterton, *The Common Man* (New York: Sheed and Ward, 1950), 56.

[15] G. K. Chesterton, *Autobiography*, *The Collected Works of G. K. Chesterton*, vol. 16 (San Francisco: Ignatius Press, 1988), 45.

In his *Autobiography*, Chesterton ponders the subject of childhood and imagination at some length. Controverting the widespread notion that children live their lives in a sort of fog of unreality, Chesterton asserted that in children can be found imagination in its purest state. Remembering his own imagination in childhood, he spoke of

> a sort of white light on everything, cutting things out very clearly, and rather emphasising their solidity. The point is that the white light had a sort of wonder in it, as if the world were as new as myself; but not that the world was anything but a real world.[16]

As children we were much more comfortable with astonishment than we are as adults, and it is our unfortunate corruption that brings us to associate wonder with unreality.

To those who argue that children are deceived by fairy tales and then damaged in being undeceived, Chesterton denied the deception in the first place. Children, he said, have no trouble in differentiating between make-believe and reality. Speaking of the toy theater that his father had built, he explained:

> I did like the toy theatre even when I knew it was a toy theatre. I did like the cardboard figures, even when I found they were of cardboard. The white light of wonder that shone on the whole business was not any sort of trick.[17]

The pure imagination of the child is neither deceived nor undeceived; it knows that make-believe is not real but that it can give "glorious glimpses into the possibilities of existence".[18]

[16] Ibid., 53.
[17] Ibid., 54.
[18] Ibid., 55.

Thus, said Chesterton, the child truly understands the nature of art. As the child knows that pretending is not deceiving, the child knows that images are not illusions. Chesterton added: "The very word images means things necessary to imagination. But not things contrary to reason; no, not even in a child. For imagination is almost the opposite of illusion."[19] Far from being the frivolous flight into unreason, then, imagination is something closer to a superior clarity that includes a childlike acceptance of the reasonableness of wonder. "It is only the grown man", Chesterton concluded, "who lives a life of make-believe and pretending; and it is he who has his head in a cloud."[20] In another context he added, "I believe that the child has inside his head a pretty correct and complete definition of the whole nature and function of art."[21]

The radical importance of these thoughts should not be overlooked. Chesterton's connection of the imagination with childlike wonder is significant, because our society tends to connect the arts with worldly sophistication, if not with urbane cynicism. True imagination, said G. K., is founded in the astonishment and wonder that results from shining that "white light" of clarity upon the objective reality. It is only corrupted adults who have taught themselves to be blind to the marvels that are all around them. Here is Chesterton's meaning when he says that "nothing is poetical if plain daylight is not poetical."[22]

During one of his trips to America, G. K. reacted to the widespread criticisms of the commercial gaudiness of the lighted street signs of Broadway. To the surprise of many, he wrote:

[19] Ibid., 56.
[20] Ibid., 58.
[21] *Common Man*, 57.
[22] G. K. Chesterton, *All Is Grist* (New York: Books for Libraries Press, 1967), 194–95.

> If a child saw these coloured lights, he would dance with as
> much delight as at any other coloured toys; and it is the duty
> of every poet, and even of every critic, to dance in respectful
> imitation of the child.[23]

Again and again in his writings, Chesterton pointed to the
child as the key to imagination. It is in the "imitation of the
child" that adults can rediscover the imagination that has been
extinguished within them.

The fact must not be overlooked that this call for poets
and critics to imitate the child is essentially a call to humility.
Indeed, Chesterton believed that humility is literally the foundation for greatness, and no less so in art than in any other
department of life. In one of his youthful poems, G. K. had
sincerely wondered how he had even managed "to earn the
reward of looking at a dandelion".[24] Later in his *Autobiography*
he recalled that childish humility as the very source of the sense
of wonder that is necessary for imagination. He wrote:

> But in substance what I said about the dandelion is exactly
> what I should say about the sunflower or the sun, or the glory
> which (as the poet said) is brighter than the sun. The only way
> to enjoy even a weed is to feel unworthy even of a weed.[25]

Here is a remarkable statement, pregnant with all of
Chesterton's doctrine of imagination. Humility—a true sense
of my unworthiness in relation to the Creator and the
created universe—is the key to wonder, the door into true
imagination.

The art of wondering bears closer examination here, because it was by far the most incessant of Chesterton's themes
in connection with imagination. In Chesterton's view,

[23] G. K. Chesterton, *What I Saw in America*, in *The Collected Works of G. K. Chesterton*, vol. 21 (San Francisco: Ignatius Press, 1990), 66.
[24] *Autobiography*, 321.
[25] Ibid.

imagination and wonder are inseparable, and the artist who does not wonder is no artist at all. Chesterton's essential point for life—and even more acutely so for art—was that one can, and ought to, choose to wonder even in the face of what is dull or ugly. Nothing, he said, is in itself boring; people choose to feel bored. Nothing is in itself prosaic; there is poetry everywhere for those with eyes to see.

"I am confident", Chesterton once wrote, "that there is no future for the modern world, unless it can understand that it has not merely to seek what is more and more exciting, but rather the yet more exciting business of discovering the excitement in things that are called dull." [26] Again, for his evidence he returned to the world of the child. In one case, he addressed the problem of waiting in a railway station—a situation of which grown-ups complain bitterly and incessantly. But Chesterton observed:

> Did you ever hear a small boy complain of having to hang about a railway station and wait for a train? No; for to him to be inside a railway station is to be inside a cavern of wonder and a palace of poetical pleasures. Because to him the red light and the green light on the signal are like a new sun and a new moon. Because to him when the wooden arm of the signal falls down suddenly, it is as if a great king had thrown down his staff as a signal and started a shrieking tournament of trains. I myself am of little boys' habit in this matter. [27]

There are other examples, such as the adventure of a man climbing the stairs in his home [28] and another essay called "The Thrills of Boredom", where G. K. recalled:

[26] G. K. Chesterton, *The Spice of Life* (Beaconsfield, Eng.: D. Finlayson, 1964), 164.

[27] G. K. Chesterton, *All Things Considered* (London: Methuen and Company, 1915), 30.

[28] G. K. Chesterton, *Alarms and Discursions* (London: Methuen and Company, 1927), 142.

a very strong and positive pleasure in being stranded in ...
unfashionable hotels, in empty waiting-rooms, or in watering-
places out of season. It seems as if we needed such places, and
sufficient solitude in them, to let certain nameless suggestions
soak into us and make a richer soil of the subconscious.[29]

This particular recollection concludes with the statement,
"The imagination can not only enjoy darkness; it can even
enjoy dullness."[30]

In Chesterton's view, then, the central problem with regard to the imagination lies in our lost ability to see the wonders that are all around us in our everyday lives. In his
Autobiography, he put it this way:

It was the problem of how men could be made to realise the
wonder and splendour of being alive, in environments which
their own daily criticism treated as dead-alive, and which
their imagination had left for dead.[31]

We have let the philosophies, habits, and demands of our
everyday lives render us blind to the miraculous and wonderful reality that is there. It is the duty of the imaginative,
said Chesterton, to help their fellow mortals rediscover the
wonder and the splendor.

As children are our natural models in the matter of fun,
humility, and wonder, so they are in the matter of nonsense.
Because children are so comfortable with nonsense—and
adults in general so uncomfortable—Chesterton explored the
world of nonsense as an aspect of imagination. In this connection he wrote:

The child has no need of nonsense: to him the whole universe is nonsensical in the noblest sense of that noble word.

[29] *All Is Grist*, 110.
[30] Ibid., 111.
[31] *Autobiography*, 132.

A tree is something top-heavy and fantastic, a donkey is as exciting as a dragon. All objects are seen through a great magnifying glass.... A child has innumerable points of inferiority ... but he has one real point of superiority. We are going forth continually to discover new aesthetic worlds, and last of all our conquests we have discovered this world of nonsense. But he has appreciated this world at a glance, and first glances are best.[32]

Why do adults struggle so to find that imaginative nonsense that is the natural world of the child? Chesterton argued that it is a form of acquired cowardice, a case of being no longer willing to take a risk. In another context he observed that "all great literary art involves the element of risk, and the greatest literary artists have commonly been those who have run the greatest risk of talking nonsense."[33]

The imagination dares to take the risks. It dares to have fun, dares to play, dares to "waste time", dares to engage in nonsense. The Christian imagination can dare because it understands in its very depths that things are not as they seem—that the first shall be last, that the smallest shall be the greatest, that the proud shall be humbled, that the little child shall lead them all. The Christian imagination knows already that the solemn tomes of academe can be as nonsensical as the rhymes of a Pobble in the Gromboolian Plain.[34] For the Christian imagination contains a measure of that divine mirth that is at once the patron of the arts and the preventer of madness.

The issue of madness was a major concern in Chesterton's works, both fiction and nonfiction. One sees as much in the very titles of some of his writings—for example, the novel

[32] *Lunacy and Letters*, 27–28.
[33] *Common Man*, 187.
[34] G. K. Chesterton, *The Defendant* (London: J. M. Dent and Sons, 1907), 67.

The Poet and the Lunatics, the essays *Lunacy and Letters*, a chapter in his *Autobiography* called "How to Be a Lunatic", and a chapter in his *Orthodoxy* called "The Maniac". Most of his novels dealt with madness in one form or another, and his most memorable protagonists were invariably deemed at least a little mad by their contemporaries. It is not surprising, then, to find that Chesterton explored the relationship between imagination and madness as well.

It was in *Orthodoxy* that G. K. gave us our best introduction to the question of madness. There he wrote: "There is a notion adrift everywhere that imagination, especially mystical imagination, is dangerous to man's mental balance. Poets are commonly spoken of as psychologically unreliable." [35] And again in his *Lunacy and Letters* he addressed the issue:

> It is sometimes said of wild and transcendental poets that they are in danger of lunacy, but their friends need in general have little fear of this. It is the prosaic people who are the commonest victims of insanity. It is the rationalists who go mad. To confess that we are living in infinity, to splash about and be carried about on the surge of infinity, is a perfectly healthy pastime, as healthy as swimming in the sea. Destruction awaits not the man who swims in the sea, but the man who tries to plumb it. [36]

Here is precisely the problem Chesterton addressed in his little play called *Magic*, the fundamental fragility of the rigidly rational-empirical mind.

It is not, G. K. argued, the imaginative people who are most at risk of going mad, for these have a propensity to tolerate the unknown, the mysterious, and the seemingly unexplainable. The minds that are most liable to crack are those

---

[35] G. K. Chesterton, *Orthodoxy*, in *The Collected Works of G. K. Chesterton*, vol. 1 (San Francisco: Ignatius Press, 1986), 218–19.
[36] *Lunacy and Letters*, 34.

that require a definite answer to every question, and prefer-
ably an answer that can be expressed in numbers. Again the
issue comes to a matter of taking a risk. The artist, said Chesterton, in order to seek the ecstasy is willing to risk the terror. G. K. wrote: "I feel, I say, like a reasonable philosophical
savage who has not allowed a mechanical chatter of words to
rob him of his natural and delightful ecstasy, of his natural
and delightful terror." [37] One of the many paradoxes of life is
that they who take themselves and their grip on reality most
seriously are those to whom madness most often comes. In
this regard Chesterton quipped:

> A lunatic is not startling to himself, because he is quite
> serious; that is what makes him a lunatic. A man who thinks
> he is a poached egg is to himself as plain as a poached
> egg.... It is only sanity that can see even a wild poetry in
> insanity. [38]

Chesterton argued that it is the poetic, or imaginative, view
of existence that keeps a person sane. "Consequently," he
concluded, "we may say truly that it is not the poets who go
mad; it is the mathematicians, the logicians, the numberers
of the stars, and the counters of the grass." [39]

Yet another common fallacy with regard to imagination,
according to Chesterton, is the notion that to be imaginative means to be constantly breaking the rules and surpassing
the limits. G. K. often spoke of "that profoundly inartistic
anarchy that objects to a limit as such." [40] He felt that the
arts were the perfect case in proving the falsity of this view.
He argued:

[37] Ibid., 71.
[38] G. K. Chesterton, *Tremendous Trifles* (New York: Dodd, Mead and Company, 1910), 98.
[39] *Lunacy and Letters*, 35.
[40] Ibid., 183.

[I]t is impossible to be an artist and not care for laws and limits. Art is limitation; the essence of every picture is the frame. If you draw a giraffe, you must draw him with a long neck. If, in your bold creative way, you hold yourself free to draw a giraffe with a short neck, you will really find that you are not free to draw a giraffe. The moment you step into a world of facts, you step into a world of limits.... The artist loves his limitations: they constitute the *thing* he is doing. The painter is glad that the canvas is flat. The sculptor is glad that the clay is colourless.[41]

The very essence of the arts, he said, is limitation, and true creativity involves delineating meaning out of the chaos of experience.

This issue of the relationship between imagination and limits was of great concern to Chesterton, because he felt that its misunderstanding was the cause of widespread mischief in the arts and in life. There is a chapter called "The Yellow Bird" in his novel *The Poet and the Lunatics* wherein a man is obsessed with the idea that the human imagination must keep breaking out of its boundaries. In the end, this imaginative anarchist carries his philosophy to its logical consequences by literally exploding himself with dynamite. The fallacy, said Chesterton, is that the imagination is a "mere longing for larger and larger horizons".[42] But Chesterton argued:

The imagination is supposed to work toward the infinite; though in that sense the infinite is the opposite of the imagination. For the imagination deals with an image, and an image is in its nature a thing that has an outline, and therefore a limit.[43]

[41] *Orthodoxy*, 243–44.
[42] *All Is Grist*, 153.
[43] Ibid.

Chesterton cited the famous poet Shelley as an example. A critic had remarked that the true poet sees the universal in everything, and had mentioned Shelley as his proof. However, G. K. flatly contradicted the claim. Speaking of the great poet he wrote:

> A deep imaginative instinct, beyond all his cheap philosophies, made him always do something which is the soul of imagination, but the very opposite of universalism. It made him *insulate* the object of which he wrote; making the cloud or the bird as solitary as possible in the sky. Imagination demands an image.... In writing of the skylark Shelley compares that unfortunate wild fowl to a lady in a tower, to a star, to a rose, to all sorts of things that are not the least like a skylark. But they all have one touch, the touch of separation and solitude.[44]

Even Shelley—the poet so famous for his rebellions against society's morals and norms—when he was doing his art could not help but invoke the limiting nature of imagination.

The significance of Chesterton's view here reached far beyond the arts. It had implications for the progressive philosophy that was so popular in his day, as it spoke against the automatic reaction that what is more and bigger and newer is always better. It had implications for the doctrines of the "free-thinkers", as it questioned the wisdom of opening the mind wider and wider without the prospect of ever closing it on something solid. It had implications for the extant moral relativism, as it refuted the lie that an absence of rules and laws is the same thing as freedom. In this regard, G. K. discussed monogamous marriage as an illustration:

> The decadents used to say that things like the marriage vow might be very convenient for commonplace public pur-

---

[44] *Spice of Life*, 37.

poses, but had no place in the world of beauty and imagination. The truth is exactly the other way. The truth is that
if marriage had not existed it would have been necessary for
artists to invent it ... it would still have been created out of
cloud and air as a poetical requirement. If ever monogamy
is abandoned in practice, it will linger in legend and in
literature.[45]

In art and in life, Chesterton claimed, there are certain "poetical requirements" that have everything to do with differ-
entiation and the setting of limits. Here is why so many varied
human societies in scattered times and places have developed
such remarkably similar moral codes and basic institutions.

The setting of limits relates closely to another aspect of
imagination—its essential nature as communication. Particularly in the realm of modern arts, it is not at all obvious that
meaningful communication is the intention of the artist. Chesterton's view on this subject was definite. He wrote:

> The artist is a person who communicates something.... But
> it is a question of communication and not merely of what
> some people call expression. Or rather, strictly speaking, un-
> less it is communication it is not expression.... The artist
> does ultimately exhibit himself as being intelligent by being
> intelligible. I do not say by being easy to understand, but
> certainly by being understood.[46]

G.K. was always rather impatient with esoterica, whether
artistic or intellectual, as he saw it as a form of snobbery
designed intentionally to exclude the common person. Here
he was particularly concerned with the propensity of modern artists to portray themselves as too "deep" to communicate

[45] G.K. Chesterton, *Fancies versus Fads* (London: Methuen and Company, 1923), 102.
[46] *Glass Walking-Stick*, 182–83.

with commoners. The true artist, he insisted, manages to communicate. In *The Glass Walking-Stick*, he complained:

> Yet there is still a vast amount of talk about the isolated and uncommunicable spirit of the man of genius; about how he has in him things too deep for expression and too subtle to be subject to general criticism. I say that that is exactly what is *not* true of the artist. That is exactly what is true of the ordinary man who is not an artist.... *He* has subtleties in his soul which he cannot describe; *he* has secrets of emotion which he can never show to the public. He it is who dies with all his music in him.[47]

Chesterton rejected the idea of the isolated and misunderstood artist on the grounds that it is the artist's job to make himself understood.

A final aspect of imagination according to Chesterton—an aspect that some will find even more surprising than the last—is that it reaches its highest form when it is dogmatic. In the broadest realms of philosophy and religion it was always Chesterton's position that the greater minds are a fountainhead of positive statements, while the lesser minds retreat into a whirlpool of negations. In the arts he felt that "if we want any art tolerably brisk and bold we have to go to the doctrinaires." [48]

Chesterton's argument here is even more impressive when we consider that he wrote in a time when the avant-garde in the arts were nearly unanimous in seeking to purge the arts of morality or doctrine of any kind. However, citing the notable cases of Rudyard Kipling and George Bernard Shaw, G. K. argued that both men's writings owed a good part of their brilliance to their passion as propaganda. In his bid to

[47] Ibid., 183.
[48] G. K. Chesterton, *Heretics*, in *The Collected Works of G. K. Chesterton*, vol. 1 (San Francisco: Ignatius Press, 1986), 199.

prove that "the fiercest dogmatists can make the best art-ists",[49] he observed:

> In the *fin de siècle* atmosphere every one was crying out that literature should be free from all causes and all ethical creeds. Art was to produce only exquisite workmanship, and it was especially the note of those days to demand brilliant plays and brilliant short stories. And when they got them, they got them from a couple of moralists. The best short stories were written by a man trying to preach Imperialism. The best plays were written by a man trying to preach Socialism. All the art of all the artists looked tiny and tedious beside the art which was a by-product of propaganda.[50]

Chesterton's remarkable claim was that the art of Kipling and Shaw was superior *because* it had a purpose. It is a matter of passion, as Chesterton went on to explain:

> The reason, indeed, is very simple. A man cannot be wise enough to be a great artist without being wise enough to wish to be a philosopher. A man cannot have the energy to produce good art without having the energy to wish to pass beyond it. A small artist is content with art; a great artist is content with nothing except everything.[51]

Great art, then, is said to come from great passion, and great passion is the result of strongly held ideas and beliefs.

Here Chesterton spoke not simply of any beliefs, as if all ideas are created equal. He spoke of an objective morality, of a positive statement of right and wrong, of a dogma. In the context of an essay discussing the morality of a Shakespear-ean play, Chesterton exclaimed sarcastically:

[49] Ibid., 197.
[50] Ibid., 197–98.
[51] Ibid., 198.

But what is all this? This is not Modern. This is not Scientific. This is not in the purely experimental and realistic manner in which Young Rebels have been writing for the last thirty or forty years. They all say they are Creative, and they ought to know. And, according to their theory of purely Creative art, there ought to be an entirely detached and unmoral attitude on the part of everybody involved. It ought not to matter whether the spot on Lady Macbeth's finger was blood or red ink; or whether she turned the multitudinous seas the colour of carnage or tomato soup.... There is nothing to be said against it; except that, if everybody were in that scientific state of mind, nobody could write *Macbeth*.[52]

In his inimitable fashion Chesterton revealed the artistic poverty that would surely result if morality were truly banished from the arts.

It is here on this final point that we return from the arts to the imagination—and particularly now to the Christian imagination. For here is clearly an aspect of imagination that reaches into the heart of the Christian artist, into the faith that gives us our hope and our purpose. If the greatest art does, indeed, spring from the passions of the doctrinaire, then the Christian artist enjoys the most substantial foundation of all. As Kipling had his Imperialism, and Shaw his Socialism, a Christian has the very Gospel of God and the unimpeachable purpose of communicating the rock of salvation to a floundering world.

Looking now in retrospect at Chesterton's comments on imagination, we find that in its every aspect the human imagination is nurtured by the Christian faith. The human being as a prodigy in nature is certainly consistent with the Christian doctrine of our special creation "in the image of God", as is the notion of our creative imaginations being divinely

---

[52] G. K. Chesterton, *All I Survey* (New York: Books for Libraries Press, 1967), 92.

endowed. The childlike propensities for fun, humor, humility, and wonder surely reflect the words of Jesus of Nazareth on the nearness of the child to the kingdom of God. The appreciation of the wonderful in the seemingly ordinary or ugly is entirely consistent with the Christian view that the more important reality is spiritual and that things are not as they may at first seem. Chesterton's comments on risks, limits, and madness cause us to recall the many times the Savior and his apostles were deemed insane by their listeners. And of course, the issue of communication points obviously to the Word, the theme of the New Testament and the very center of the Christian faith.

In the end, Chesterton believed that for the Christian, the purpose of art is to help people to discover the glory they have lost. As fallen and flawed images of the eternal Creator we retain in our imaginations that faint echo or fleeting memory of what is wonderful and grand. Chesterton said it this way:

> At the back of our brains, so to speak, there was a forgotten blaze or burst of astonishment at our own existence. The object of the artistic and spiritual life was to dig for this submerged sunrise of wonder.[53]

[53] *Autobiography*, 97.

Chapter Three

Prigs, Critics, and Other Nuisances

God, the Creator of all things, created the human species with very special endowments in God's own image. Not of the least importance among these endowments is a measure of creativity and an active imagination. However, Christian doctrine holds that humanity has subsequently fallen into a degraded state in which the vestiges of the divine attributes have been all but obliterated. Though the human propensity to imagination remains, humanity tends in its thoughts, actions, habits, and institutions to stifle, stultify, pervert, and even extinguish the free play of imagination.

In his lifetime, G. K. Chesterton recognized these forces that are so inimical to imagination, and he opposed them with a passion worthy of the title of "the Wild Knight" by which he came to be known. In this chapter we follow this great Christian and artist as he explores the various enemies of imagination, paying particular attention to the creative arts, the artists themselves, and the subcultures of various people who have much to do with the state of the arts. In Chesterton's view, to ponder the things that inhibit the imagination and the arts is to understand more clearly the power that seeks to steal the faith and hope and joy that are the intended birthright of every child of God.

The greatest threat to imagination, according to Chesterton, is the popular philosophical view that he calls materialism—the notion that all entities with any claim to reality are derived ultimately from material phenomena. "There is something strange", G. K. once wrote, "in the modern mind, by which a material cause always seems more like a real cause." [1] Descending directly from materialist philosophy are the ideas of scientific positivism and the missionary zeal of the cult of scientism. While much of the best work in the sciences involves the active use of imagination, Chesterton argued passionately against the mind-deadening determinisms that eventually crept into popular scientific thought.

In a delightful essay called "The Wind and the Trees", Chesterton illustrated the basic materialist point of view by recalling a windy day in the park. He was sitting under some trees, he said, "with a great wind boiling like surf about the tops of them, so that their living load of leaves rocks and roars in something that is at once exultation and agony". [2] At this sight Chesterton recalled:

> I remember a little boy of my acquaintance who was once walking in Battersea Park under just such torn skies and tossing trees. He did not like the wind at all; it blew in his face too much; it made him shut his eyes; it blew off his hat, of which he was very proud. He was, as far as I remember, about four. After complaining repeatedly of the atmospheric unrest, he said at last to his mother, "Well, why don't you take away the trees, and then it wouldn't wind." [3]

Chesterton went on to concede that nothing could be more natural than the mistake of thinking that the trees were like

[1] G. K. Chesterton, *All I Survey* (New York: Books for Libraries Press, 1967), 175.
[2] G. K. Chesterton, *Tremendous Trifles* (New York: Dodd, Mead and Company, 1910), 69.
[3] Ibid., 69–70.

giant fans that were responsible for stirring up the wind. In this vein he added:

> Indeed, the belief is so human and excusable that it is, as a matter of fact, the belief of about ninety-nine of a hundred of the philosophers, reformers, sociologists, and politicians of the great age in which we live. My small friend was, in fact, very like the principal modern thinkers; only much nicer.[4]

Materialism is the idea that what is visible is the cause of what is invisible—that the material world is what is "real" and everything else is merely derivative from the material. Thought, for example, is a result of the movement of atoms in brain tissue. "The great human heresy", Chesterton said figuratively, "is that the trees move the wind."[5] The great lie is "that the material circumstances have alone created the moral circumstances".[6]

Among the many deleterious consequences of this popular materialist philosophy, said Chesterton, is that the accepted notion of "realism" becomes necessarily prosaic and dull. "Realism", he wrote, "means that the world is dull and full of routine, but that the soul is sick and screaming."[7] Where the more imaginative person may see "that the universe is wild and full of wonders",[8] the materialist is blinded by a cloud of "realism". G. K. explained:

> Another way of explaining the cloud of commonplace interpretation upon modern things is to trace it to that spirit which often calls itself science but which is more often mere repetition. It is proverbial that a child looking out of the

[4] Ibid., 70–72.
[5] Ibid., 72.
[6] Ibid.
[7] Ibid., 97.
[8] Ibid., 69.

nursery window, regards the lamp-post as part of a fairy-tale
of which the lamplighter is the fairy. The lamp-post can be
to a baby all that the moon could possibly be to a lover or a
poet. Now it is perfectly true that there is nowadays a spirit
of cheap information which imagines that it shoots beyond
this shining point, when it merely tells us that there are nine
hundred lamp-posts in the town, all exactly alike.... And
we can say ... that there is nothing really commonplace except the mind of the calculator. The baby is much more
right about the flaming lamp than the statistician who counts
the posts in the street; and the lover is much more really
right about the moon than the astronomer. Here the part is
certainly greater than the whole, for it is much better to
be tied to one wonderful thing than to allow a mere catalogue of wonderful things to deprive you of the capacity to
wonder.[9]

This final sentence contains the gist of Chesterton's objection to the cult of scientism. If scientific facts and figures
produce the net result of robbing the world of its wonder,
then the price for such "knowledge" is far too dear.

Such a dulling of the natural sense of wonder was, in Chesterton's view, the actual result of scientism in the latter part
of the nineteenth century. The Victorians, he said,

had a very real and even childlike wonder at things like the
steam-engine or the telephone, considered as toys. Unfortunately the long result of time, on the fairy-tales of science,
has been to extend the science and lessen the fairy-tale, that
is, the sense of the fairy-tale.[10]

It was important to G.K. that people understood that his
objection was not to science itself but to the deadening of

[9] G.K. Chesterton, *The Uses of Diversity* (New York: Dodd, Mead and
Company, 1921), 12–13.
[10] G.K. Chesterton, *Fancies versus Fads* (London: Methuen and Company,
1923), 209.

the imagination that people too often derived from their notions of scientific explanation. This is a point that he explained clearly:

> Let it be noted that this is *not*, as is always loosely imagined, a reaction against material science; or a regret for mechanical invention; or a depreciation of telephones or telescopes or anything else. It is exactly the other way. I am not depreciating telephones; I am complaining that they are not appreciated. I am not attacking inventions; I am attacking indifference to inventions. I only remark that it is the same people who brag about them who are really indifferent to them. I am not objecting to the statement that the science of the modern world is wonderful; I am only objecting to the modern world because it does not wonder at it.[11]

The scientific and technological wonders are surely products—at least in part—of the imagination, but Chesterton objected to their use as a destroyer of the imagination.

One of the great ironies that Chesterton pointed out with regard to the dulling effect of this materialist point of view is that its foundations lie in the philosophical tradition called the Enlightenment. Playing on the imagery suggesting that enlightenment ought to make things brighter and clearer, G. K. examined the case of a scientific man who could find no interest in an album containing his grandfather's cavalry charge at Balaclava. Chesterton wrote of such a man:

> We must now suppose that he has drifted into a dull mood, in which somebody sitting on a horse means no more than somebody sitting on a chair.... His grandfather's charge at Balaclava seem to him as dull and dusty as the album containing such family portraits. Such a person has not really

[11] G. K. Chesterton, *As I Was Saying* (New York: Books for Libraries Press, 1966), 185.

become enlightened about the album; on the contrary, he
has only become blind with the dust.[12]

This dullness is not native to us; it is something we acquire
by learning to look at the world in a certain way—the Enlightenment way, the materialist way, the quantitative way,
the way of scientism.

However, consistent with his thoroughly Romantic view,
Chesterton asserted that the human being is much more than
merely a perceiving and thinking animal. There is the whole
realm of the spirit and of the creative imagination, which
defines humanity even more clearly than does mere intelligence. This realm is something of which we are at least vaguely
conscious, even when we have managed to extinguish the
greater part of its expression in our thoughts and lives. It is
something that we can remember if we really try. G. K. put
it this way:

> We are all under the same mental calamity; we have all for-
> gotten our names. We have all forgotten what we really are.
> All that we call common sense and rationality and practical-
> ity and positivism only means that for certain dead levels of
> our life we forget that we have forgotten. All that we call
> spirit and art and ecstasy only means that for one awful in-
> stant we remember that we forget.[13]

In our world we grope in a cloud that hides from us who we
really are. Our religion and our arts are our attempts to find
again what it is that we have lost.

That the problem is we, ourselves, and not the world around
us, was a point essential to Chesterton's arguments. In fact,
this notion became the dominant theme in his writings, his

[12] G. K. Chesterton, *The Everlasting Man*, in *The Collected Works of G. K. Chesterton*, vol. 2 (San Francisco: Ignatius Press, 1986),149.

[13] G. K. Chesterton, *Orthodoxy*, in *The Collected Works of G. K. Chesterton*, vol. 1 (San Francisco: Ignatius Press, 1986), 257.

religion, and his life. The issue is so very important to an understanding of Chesterton's views on imagination that a rather lengthy quotation on the matter is here reported in full. In *The Common Man*, G. K. wrote:

> After all, what could be more mystical or magical than ordinary daylight coming in through an ordinary window? ... Why should not that wonderful white fire breaking through the window, inspire us every day like an ever-returning miracle? ... And the more I thought of it, the more I thought that there was the hint of some strange answer in the very fact that I had to ask the question. I had not lost, and I have never lost, the conviction that such primal things are mysterious and amazing. Why did anybody have to remind us that they were amazing? Why was there ... a sort of daily fight to appreciate the daylight; to which we had to summon all the imagination and poetry and labour of the arts to aid us? If the first imaginative instinct was right, it seemed clearer and clearer that something else was wrong. And as I indignantly denied that there was anything wrong with the window, I eventually concluded that there was something wrong with me.[14]

In Chesterton's view the greatest enemy of imagination is that pervasive and powerful materialism that through its day-to-day "realism" rocks us into a state of blind stupor. Our eyesight is so damaged that we are scarcely able to see anymore the wonders and miracles that exist and take place all around us. The primary business of the Christian imagination is to aid us in learning to appreciate again those mysterious and amazing things we once knew.

Despite Chesterton's earlier disclaimer that he had nothing against science itself, he had plenty to say in opposition to those early anthropological studies that made so much of

[14] G. K. Chesterton, *The Common Man* (New York: Sheed and Ward, 1950), 242–43.

being the "science of man". In fact, one of his major non-fiction works, *The Everlasting Man*, consisted almost entirely of a critique and arguments over the claims of anthropology regarding the origins and nature of humans. His initial charge was that the relevant "facts" of the scholars were not facts at all but rather assumptions and speculations based on extremely flimsy evidence. Perhaps even more important was his observation that in taking the narrow view of the natural sciences, the anthropologists had managed to construct a picture of humanity that left out the most important human characteristics of all. The result was a compendium of fussy speculations about ancient people, as if their lives consisted of nothing but normative behavior and irrational myths and superstitions.

Chesterton complained that there came to be a telling predictability in those early ethnographies, reflecting a rather condescending analysis of what people were ostensibly like before the advent of Civilization and Enlightenment. There came to be too much talk of totemism and fertility rites and propitiations to the gods. As G. K. put it in *The Everlasting Man*:

> The true origin of all the myths has been discovered much too often. There are too many keys to mythology.... Everything is phallic; everything is totemistic; everything is seed-time and harvest; everything is ghosts and grave-offerings; everything is the golden bough of sacrifice; everything is the sun and moon.... Yet the whole trouble comes from a man trying to look at these stories from the outside, as if they were scientific objects.[15]

These tiresome tales of pre-history, Chesterton argued, were the result of a narrowly prescribed point of view on the nature of the human being. Viewing the human creature in its

[15] *Everlasting Man*, 235.

entirety—that is, including not only its rational mind but also its imagination and spirit—yields a great many other explanations that are both as plausible and as supportable by facts as those of the scholarly experts.

Again Chesterton accused the pre-historians of an atheistic bias so strong as to blind them to the obvious meanings of their own data. For example, the scholars went to great lengths to praise and ponder the pictures found on cave walls, yet they seemed obstinately to resist the logical conclusion about the nature of humanity. Chesterton argued:

> We must all, by this time, be familiar with the expressions of admiration for the art of the cavemen.... The further we go back to explore, the more we find that is really worth exploring; and the nearer we are to the real primitive man, the further we are from either the ape or even the savage.[16]

The pivotal fact that Chesterton was unwilling to let the scholars sweep under the rug of their evolutionary theories is that the evidence reveals pre-historic humans who were vastly different from the other animals by virtue of their active imaginations.

Chesterton's final word in contradiction of the materialist view was balanced, however, by his strong assertion against the polar opposite view—that *nothing* is material, or that reality consists in perceptions and nothing more. The Christian imagination accepts the reality of both the material and the metaphysical, both the flesh and the spirit. In his book on Thomas Aquinas, Chesterton explained a Christian view of mind and imagination:

> Note how this view avoids both pitfalls; the alternative abysses of impotence. The mind is not merely receptive, in the sense that it absorbs sensations like so much blotting-paper; on

[16] *Common Man,* 100.

that sort of softness has been based all that cowardly materialism, which conceives man as wholly servile to his environment. On the other hand, the mind is not purely creative, in the sense that it paints pictures on the windows and then mistakes them for a landscape outside. But the mind is active, and its activity consists in following, so far as the will chooses to follow, the light outside that does really shine upon real landscapes. That is what gives the undefinably virile and even adventurous quality to this view of life; as compared with that which holds that material influences pour in upon an utterly helpless mind, or that which holds that psychological influences pour out and create an entirely baseless phantasmagoria.[17]

Among the greatest enemies of the Christian imagination, then, are the determinisms that rob the human creature of its ability to encounter what is real and to play a hand in shaping it. In Chesterton's view, both of the "alternative abysses of impotence" are an attempt to convince the "images of God" that their thoughts and behaviors—including their religion and their arts—are determined either by material, social, and economic forces outside them or by psycho-biological forces inside them. Chesterton argued that humans are obviously both creatures and creators, being subject to material phenomena and yet able to think and imagine and create as well. To accept a deterministic theory of humanity, G. K. concluded, is to abdicate the glory of the *imago Dei* and to relinquish those God-given endowments that define us as uniquely human creatures.

Turning to a more sociological level, Chesterton also had a great deal to say about the stultifying influences—on the imagination in general and the arts in particular—of what he indelicately called "prigs" and "snobs" and sometimes

[17] G. K. Chesterton, *Saint Thomas Aquinas*, in *The Collected Works of G. K. Chesterton*, vol. 2 (San Francisco: Ignatius Press, 1986), 542.

"aesthetes". Here he moved his focus from the greater philosophical milieu to the more specific issue of people's behavior. What are the forces, he asked, within and surrounding the arts that actually work to impede the free exercise and expression of the imagination? Few will be surprised that the most fundamental culprit was pride.

In an amusing definition of the difference between snobs and prigs, G. K. wrote: "[T]his class has split up into the two great sections of Snobs and Prigs. The first are those who want to get into Society; the second are those who want to get out of Society, and into Societies." [18] With regard to the arts, Chesterton differentiated clearly between the artist and the aesthete[19]—the "arty" kind of person who makes a show of his involvement with the arts. Of the aesthetes Chesterton wrote:

> They have goaded and jaded their artistic feelings too much to enjoy anything simply beautiful. They are aesthetes; and the definition of an aesthete is a man who is experienced enough to admire a good picture, but not inexperienced enough to see it.[20]

Here Chesterton was talking about people who are interested in "art for art's sake"[21] but who have become so jaded as to be unable to appreciate the actual expression of the artist.

In his book *Heretics*, Chesterton wrote:

> Any man with a vital knowledge of the human psychology ought to have the most profound suspicion of anybody who

[18] G. K. Chesterton, *Autobiography*, *The Collected Works of G. K. Chesterton*, vol. 16 (San Francisco: Ignatius Press, 1988), 27.

[19] Ibid., 269.

[20] G. K. Chesterton, *Lunacy and Letters* (New York: Sheed and Ward, 1958), 92.

[21] G. K. Chesterton, *Heretics*, in *The Collected Works of G. K. Chesterton*, vol. 1 (San Francisco: Ignatius Press, 1986), 42.

claims to be an artist, and talks a great deal about art. Art is
a right and human thing, like walking or saying one's prayers;
but the moment it begins to be talked about very solemnly,
a man may be fairly certain that the thing has come into a
congestion and a kind of difficulty.[22]

Chesterton held that excessive talk about one's art becomes
a kind of "congestion" to the natural flow of the imagination. Perhaps it is an oversimplification to say so, but G. K.
was really referring to the difference between doing and talking about doing.

It is obvious, though, that Chesterton was troubled not so
much by an artist speaking sincerely about his craft but by
the whole subculture of aesthetes whose intention seemed
to be pose and posture as artistic types. In this regard he
often spoke of "the artistic temperament", which he considered a plague to the imagination. G. K. explained:

The artistic temperament is a disease that afflicts amateurs.
It is a disease which arises from men not having sufficient
power of expression to utter and get rid of the element of
art in their being. It is healthful to every sane man to utter
the art within him; it is essential to every sane man to get
rid of the art within him at all costs. Artists of a large and
wholesome vitality get rid of their art easily, as they breathe
easily, or perspire easily. But in artists of less force, the thing
becomes a pressure, and produces a definite pain, which is
called the artistic temperament. Thus, the very great artists
are able to be ordinary men—men like Shakespeare or
Browning. There are many real tragedies of the artistic temperament, tragedies of vanity or violence or fear. But the
great tragedy of the artistic temperament is that it cannot
produce any art.[23]

[22] Ibid., 171.
[23] Ibid., 171.

Chesterton insisted that real artists are ordinary people who do art; they are not finely tuned instruments hovering on the brink of psychological catastrophe. Nor do artists need to live in trendy places, to possess certain eccentric furnishings, to wear a certain arty kind of clothing, or to eat at certain notorious cafés. Aesthetes, however, must be careful about such matters.

In describing his own home and family, G. K. said that "our dress and furniture were as yet untouched by anything 'arty,' in spite of a quite decently informed interest in art." [24] In another context he referred to "those ragged or ridiculous or affected artistic costumes" [25] of the aesthetes, as opposed to himself and the other artists of his acquaintance. "We were careless in wearing careful clothes", he observed. Then he added, "The aesthetes were careful in wearing careless clothes.... The Bohemian wore a slouch-hat; but he did not slouch in it." [26]

The Bohemian life-style was not an issue to Chesterton one way or the other, except when it appeared to be a self-conscious attempt to seem "arty". However, in his day when people were making such a big deal about Bohemianism as a positive virtue, G. K. could not resist a little play with the terminology itself:

> I remember when it was announced that Bohemia was to cease to exist.... It was to be called Czechoslovakia; and I went around asking people in Fleet Street whether this change was to be applied to the metaphorical Bohemia of our own romantic youth. When the wild son disturbed the respectable household, was it to be said, "I wish Tom would get out of his Czechoslovakian ways," or, when Fleet

[24] *Autobiography*, 133.
[25] Ibid., 144.
[26] Ibid., 134.

Street grew riotous, "I hate these rowdy Czechoslovakian parties." [27]

In his poetry collection called *Greybeards at Play*, Chesterton wrote a piece called "On the Disastrous Spread of Aestheticism in All Classes". There he lampooned aestheticism as a hobby that only an idle and nonessential class can afford to indulge in. He began with some lines depicting the working class seized by the artistic temperament. For example:

> The Shopmen, when their souls were still,
> Declined to open shop—
> And Cooks recorded frames of mind
> In sad and subtle chops.[28]

The poem goes on as such, showing the aesthetic urge spreading broadly through society and nature, until finally:

> The sun had read a little book
> That struck him with a notion:
> He drowned himself and all his fires
> Deep in the hissing ocean.[29]

In the end, Chesterton was saying that if all of the self-indulgent artiness were to spread too far, the result would mean an end not only of the truly imaginative arts but of everything else as well.

This seemingly extreme position derived from Chesterton's passionate war against the pessimistic philosophies that were in vogue in those days. During his youth at the Slade School of Art, he had encountered a cult of rather nihilistic hedonists, and the aesthetes in general tended toward an amoral, pessimistic, seize-the-moment kind of doctrine. Ches-

[27] Ibid., 178.
[28] G. K. Chesterton, *Greybeards at Play* (London: Elek, 1974), 43–44.
[29] Ibid., 47.

terton felt that such nihilism and pessimism are among the greatest nemeses to the free and fruitful imagination. In his book *Heretics*, he explained:

> In this cult of the pessimistic pleasure-seeker ... many of the most brilliant intellects of our time have urged us to the same self-conscious snatching at a rare delight.... [T]hat we were all under the sentence of death, and the only course was to enjoy exquisite moments simply for those moments' sake.... It is the *carpe diem* religion; but the *carpe diem* religion is not the religion of happy people, but of very unhappy people. Great joy does not gather the rosebuds while it may; its eyes are fixed on the immortal rose which Dante saw. Great joy has in it the sense of immortality.... No blow then has ever been struck at the natural loves and laughter of men so sterilizing as this *carpe diem* of the aesthetes.[30]

One sees here the fundamental opposition between the natural joy underlying the Christian imagination and the transitory and almost desperate happiness of the aesthete.

Another habit of the aesthetes that Chesterton considered deleterious to the imagination and the arts was the pell-mell pursuit of artistic fads and fashions. In *Lunacy and Letters*, G.K. referred to early Victorian times as "an age which really believed ... that the function of art meant something else than keeping pace with French book-covers".[31] In another context he added even more sharply: "But, then, aesthetes never do anything but what they are told. When they heard that pewter was beautiful they rushed out and bought all the pewter mugs out of the public-houses."[32] If these comments seem a bit petty, it must be noted that they reflect a larger and more legitimate concern that artistic fads and "schools" and conventions unnecessarily limit the field of

[30] *Heretics*, 94–95.
[31] *Lunacy and Letters*, 54.
[32] Ibid., 160.

imaginative expression. As long, argued Chesterton, as artists limit themselves to using only the forms and methods dictated by the fashions of their particular time and place, they are letting mere convention stifle their imagination. Few would disagree with this statement as it relates to inventing *new* forms of expression; but Chesterton always argued that the principle is the same for the past as well. Subjects and styles that were popular in times past ought not, he insisted, be eliminated from the imaginative possibilities of the present.

Another major killer of the imagination, according to Chesterton, is the corrupting influence of success itself—speaking both societally and personally. The ancient proverb saying that pride comes before a fall is no less true for the imaginative artist than for anyone else. G. K. often spoke of the deadening influences of urban-industrial life. For example, in a discussion of why the Irish seem to love poetry more than the English do, he wrote:

> There is nothing Celtic about loving poetry; the English loved poetry more, perhaps, than any other people before they came under the shadow of the chimney-pot and the shadow of the chimney-pot hat. . . . In all this the Irish are simply an ordinary nation which has not been either sodden with smoke or oppressed by money-lenders, or otherwise corrupted with wealth and science.[33]

Chesterton insisted that the commercial state of mind can corrupt and co-opt the imagination, and he felt that the extant gaudy advertising would make the task of the imaginative artist much more difficult. In this connection, he wrote:

> When at last people see—as at the Pageant—crosses and dragons, leopards and lilies, there is scarcely one of the things that they now see as a symbol which they have not already

---

[33] *Heretics*, 135 (order of quotations reversed).

seen as a trade-mark. If the great "Assumption of the Virgin" were painted in front of them they might remember Blank's Blue. If the Emperor of China were buried before them, the yellow robes might remind them of Dash's Mustard. We have not the task of preaching colour and gaiety to a people who has never had it.... We have a harder task. We have to teach those to appreciate it who have always seen it.[34]

It may seem like exaggeration to say that the painter who uses yellow will find it difficult to evoke a response other than the thought of Dash's Mustard, but Chesterton sought to illustrate the point that such things as nuance and subtlety were being driven from the field by advertising.

Again his concern was the forces that decrease our ability to appreciate, to enjoy, to wonder—the influences that kill the imagination. In *The Defendant*, G. K. described the educated classes as "cloyed and demoralised with the mere indulgence of art and mood".[35] There are ways, he observed, in which the uneducated possess the distinct advantage of being able to enjoy the commonplace and trivial, while those of more discriminating taste find less that can capture their jaded imaginations. Chesterton wrote:

> The merely educated can scarcely ever be brought to believe that this world is itself an interesting place. When they look at a work of art ... they expect to be interested, but when they look at a newspaper advertisement or a group in the street, they do not ... expect to be interested. But to common and simple people this world is a work of art, though it is, like many great works of art, anonymous. They look to life for interest with the same kind of cheerful and uneradicable assurance with which we look for interest at a comedy for which we have paid money at the door. To the eyes of

[34] *Uses of Diversity*, 130–31.
[35] G. K. Chesterton, *The Defendant* (London: J. M. Dent and Sons, 1907), 99.

the ultimate school of contemporary fastidiousness, the universe is indeed an ill-drawn and over-coloured picture, the
scrawlings in circles of a baby upon the slate of night; its
starry skies are a vulgar pattern which they would not have
for a wallpaper, its flowers and fruits have a cockney bril-
liancy, like the holiday hat of a flower-girl.[36]

In other words, sophistication has its costs, and not the least
of these is the dulling of the imagination.

For the artist, argued Chesterton, the most deadly of all
enemies to the imagination is the pride that follows so naturally upon the heels of success. For the Christian artist the
calamity is even greater, because the Christian is called to
avoid personal glory and to give all praise to God, the Author and Creator of all that is good. Again using the word
poet to mean imaginative artists of all kinds, Chesterton made
one of his most important observations concerning the arts:

It is wholesome to note that the poet generally came a crop-
per when he was moving most smoothly on the butter-slide
of praise and progress and the prevailing fashion. It is when
the classical poet is most classical that he strikes us as pompous and vapid. It is when the romantic poet is most romantic
that he strikes us as sloppy and sentimental. And it will be
when the modern poet is most modern ... that he will strike
posterity as merely dowdy and dull.[37]

In other words, history shows us that the proverb is true.
Success can be a dangerous killer, because it is the "butter-
slide" into pride.

Here we have followed G. K. Chesterton to his most essential point. True imagination—and most especially Christian imagination—is grounded solidly in the soil of humility.
Here is why pridefulness has such an extinguishing effect on

[36] Ibid., 97–98.
[37] *All I Survey*, 74.

the imaginative processes. Pride is directly inimical to creativity. In his masterpiece *Orthodoxy*, Chesterton explained:

> Humility was largely meant as a restraint upon the arrogance and infinity of the appetite of man. He was always outstripping his mercies with his own newly invented needs. His very power of enjoyment destroyed half his joys. By asking for pleasure, he lost the chief pleasure; for the chief pleasure is surprise. Hence it became evident that if a man would make his world large, he must be always making himself small. Even the haughty visions, the tall cities, and the toppling pinnacles are the creations of humility. Giants that tread down forests like grass are the creations of humility. Towers that vanish upwards above the loneliest star are the creations of humility. For towers are not tall unless we look up at them; and giants are not giants unless they are larger than we. All this gigantesque imagination, which is, perhaps, the mightiest of the pleasures of man, is at bottom entirely humble.[38]

If in our arts we would make the world large, we must make ourselves small. If we harbor even the most secret notions of our own greatness, then we cannot be surprised to find that our imagination becomes congested and cold. It is the very law of imagination written by the greatest Creator of all.

Finally, Chesterton saved some of his most acerbic rhetoric for those perennial commentators on the arts—the critics. Concerning the critics, G. K. had a great deal to say, but his observations can be divided into four general issues: their bias against morality in the arts, their unreflecting progressivism, their incessantly negative orientation, and their propensity to faddishness.

By the end of the nineteenth century there had grown an intellectual subculture in Western Europe and North America

[38] *Orthodoxy*, 234.

that sought to purge society—and particularly the arts—of anything resembling traditional morality. The popular philosophy of the day held that all moral ideas were simple cultural artifacts and that their validity was therefore merely relative to situations. Given this opinion, those people, who considered themselves the very most clever and in-the-know, placed themselves above all morality. This view was particularly popular in the world of artistic criticism. Chesterton, however, reacted thus:

> The bias against morality among the modern aesthetes is a thing very much paraded.... The modern aesthete wishing us to believe that he values beauty more than conduct, reads Mallarmé, and drinks absinthe in a tavern. But this is not only his favourite kind of beauty; it is also his favourite kind of conduct. If he really wished us to believe that he cared for beauty only, he ought to go to nothing but Wesleyan school treats, and paint the sunlight in the hair of the Wesleyan babies.[39]

Chesterton pointed out that the people who were so busy posturing their amoral and anarchic ideas were in reality conformists to a rather strong set of alternative—even if unrecognized—morals of their own. In fact, these ostensible nonconformists limited themselves to a narrower range of behavior, even to the extent of enforcing what is acceptable to read and to drink.

Likewise, moral relativism had become the only acceptable creed, as the liberal urge calcified into liberal dogma. What Chesterton found most objectionable in relativism was that it was not so much a case of toleration for the views of others as it was a categorical rejection of all positive ideas as a matter of principle. "It is the new orthodoxy", he once

[39] *Heretics*, 168.

wrote, "that a man may be uncertain of everything; so long as he is not certain of anything." [40]

Particularly in the arts, Chesterton felt that this unreasoning bias against morality had a definitely harmful effect on the imagination. Recall his earlier observation that Kipling and Shaw, two of the finest Victorian writers, were both moralists through and through. In *The Glass Walking-Stick*, Chesterton complained about moral relativism in the artistic critic:

> He will tell us that a pool with green scum on it partly depressed and partly delighted him; but he will not *decide*; he will not pronounce upon whether there ought to be any pond; or whether any pond ought to have any scum; or whether any scum ought to be green or peacock-blue; or whether, in short, he thanks God for a good green pond, or merely feels inclined to drown himself in it. [41]

Clearly, Chesterton was exasperated to see the arts becoming so entangled in their amoral biases as to render them impotent and insipid.

Chesterton's second complaint against the critics was their unreflecting adherence to progressive doctrine. The problem, said Chesterton, with progressivism is that it begs the question as to whether things are getting better or worse. The progressive always assumes that change is for the better. This doctrine is an essentially self-congratulatory one, in that whatever we happen to be doing at the present time is deemed superior to everything that was done in the past. In the arts this idea leads to novelty for novelty's sake and to a necessarily negative opinion on anything conventional. The very

[40] G. K. Chesterton, *The Glass Walking-Stick* (London: Methuen and Company, 1955), 178.

[41] Ibid., 177.

word *traditional* becomes a derogatory term. In *The Common Man*, G. K. wrote:

> I mean that modern men are not familiar with the rational arguments for tradition; but they are familiar, and most wearily familiar, with the rational arguments for change ... the whole modern world is verbally prepared to regard the new artist as right and the old artist as wrong. It is prepared to do so by the whole progressive philosophy; which is often rather a phraseology than a philosophy.[42]

The critics, said Chesterton, are always ready to pronounce a work outdated or out-of-step with the trends, as if such a comment were artistically relevant or even useful information. Whenever the artist is concerned with being on the cutting-edge of artistic progress, the imagination takes the back seat.

In his art as in his philosophy, Chesterton fiercely defended his right to embrace old ideas and traditional methods. When the progressives tried to relegate all past things to the proverbial dumpster of history, G. K. argued the point that many traditions happen to contain important truths. To paraphrase one of his remarks, he once said that the progressives claimed that a thing that is valid on Tuesday cannot be valid on Thursday. Although it was the relativists and progressives who made the most noise about being "free-thinkers", Chesterton argued that the truly free mind is also open to the possibility that something traditional might actually be true.

Chesterton was always quick to defend the artist whom the critics charged with being out-of-date. For example, he once wrote: "The carping critics who have abused Tennyson for this do not see that it was far more daring and orig-

---

[42] *Common Man*, 112.

inal for a poet to defend conventionality than to defend a cart-load of revolutions."[43] And similarly, about a certain critic: "He is only a very shallow critic who cannot see an eternal rebel in the heart of a Conservative."[44] Chesterton's point, of course, was not that conservatism is always better than liberalism, nor that the old way is always better than the new; but that each case ought to be judged on its own, internal merits.

The third objection that Chesterton raised against the critics of his day concerned their incessant negativism. Rather than to approach a work of art with the purpose of appreciating it on its own terms, the critic too often simply looks for the flaws. In literature, for example, G. K. said that typically "the critic skims an ordinary anthology to find an item which he can condemn as a blemish"[45] and, in doing so, fails to engage the meaning of the whole piece.

Regarding the relationship between a critic and a work of art, Chesterton wrote:

> I would not say that the excellent and sometimes exquisite critics of more recent times are dead or buriable; but I do say that their type of criticism necessarily misses the very meaning and purpose of those direct appeals.... In this case there is a real meaning in the modern substitution of the word "appreciation" for the word "criticism." These are not things that we criticize, but things which we appreciate—or do not appreciate. But those who depreciate, because they cannot appreciate, are simple people who have got hold of the wrong subject for their particular sort of appreciation.[46]

[43] G. K. Chesterton, *Varied Types* (New York: Dodd, Mead and Company, 1903), 255.

[44] Ibid., 252.

[45] *All I Survey*, 69–70.

[46] G. K. Chesterton, *Generally Speaking* (New York: Dodd, Mead and Company, 1929), 272.

In order to speak intelligently and fairly, the critic must first learn to appreciate—that is not the same thing as to like or to praise—the work of art. Far too often the critic sees his role as necessarily to depreciate a work even without really understanding it.

One popular way to depreciate a work of art is to question its originality. Attached to every genre there are critics who thrive on pointing out that one work of art seems to "reflect" or "echo" or "shadow" or "be influenced by" another work of art. In this regard Chesterton wrote:

> In almost all the cases I come across, the resemblance between one passage and another, suggested by the ingenious critic, is really not a resemblance at all, let alone an artificial or suspicious resemblance. There is no reason why two independent poets should not think of the same image or idea quite independently.... The critic insists that one poet is "indebted" to the other ... but I protest when they prove his literary thieving by quoting "Where are the snows of yesteryear?" and then giving a list of all the poets who had previously mentioned snow.[47]

The real crime, said Chesterton, is that in pursuing such dubious comparisons the critic more times than not fails even to address the substance of the art itself. The result is a merely superficial look at the piece, omitting the most important information of all. "There is something about the mood of the critic who finds comparisons," Chesterton wrote, "something eager and hasty and superficially satisfied, which prevents them ... from really considering what the poet says."[48] In *Come to Think of It*, he added: "It seems to me common sense to leave original poets alone with their original ideas,

[47] G. K. Chesterton, *Come to Think of It* (London: Methuen and Company, 1930), 18–19.
[48] Ibid., 19.

and not strain logic and language to cracking in order to prove that they are not original." [49]

Another negative theme among the critics was the popular disparagement of what they called "pretty" in the visual arts. The thoroughly modern artist was not supposed to make pictures that were pretty. Prettiness was considered a thing of the past or, even worse, an appeal to the sentimentalism of the lower classes. Against such snobbery, G. K. argued:

> For a child has a very sound sense of wonder at what is really wonderful; and by no means merely a vulgar or varnished taste in what is conventionally beautiful.... Children are not snobs in art any more than in morals. And if they often have also a pleasure in things that are really "pretty" ... it is simply because there is a perfectly legitimate place in art for what is pretty. [50]

Thus, again Chesterton returned to the childlike sense of wonder as the measuring rod for the arts and imagination. Here, however, he extended the criterion to include artistic criticism as well. He wrote, "This is the beginning of all sane art criticism: wonder combined with the complete serenity of the conscience in the acceptance of such wonders." [51]

Part of the problem of negativism among the critics is grounded in a larger issue of language. Chesterton observed that our language tends to contain more negative terms than positive ones, and particularly the standard language of criticism reveals a paucity of appreciative language. For example, with regard to the criticism of poetry, Chesterton observed that "one of the first facts which a good poetical critic will

[49] Ibid., 22.
[50] *Common Man*, 114.
[51] Ibid., 57.

realise, is one which the poet of necessity realises: the limitation of language, and especially the poverty and clumsiness of
the language of praise." [52] However, Chesterton considered it
the duty of good critics to develop a critical language capable
of affirmation and even admiration as well as derogation.

In the end Chesterton reminded the critics of their re-
sponsibility not only to the artists but to the readers of their
critiques. At the very least, the readers want information about
the actual content of the piece of art. They would also primarily want to know of its merits, and only secondarily of
its flaws. In this regard Chesterton wrote:

> The supreme business of criticism is to discover the part of a
> man's work which is his and to ignore that part which be-
> longs to others. Why should any critic of poetry spend time
> and attention on that part of a man's work which is unpo-
> etical? Why should any man be interested in aspects which
> are uninteresting? The business of a critic is to discover the
> importance of men and not their crimes. [53]

Is anyone really fascinated by a critic's statement of how un-
original something is or how badly it is done? The critic's
real challenge, said Chesterton, is to help the public understand and interpret the work of the artists.

The final charge that G. K. Chesterton leveled against the
critics concerned their propensity to faddishness. There is
always a tendency for a subculture to grow among the more
famous critics, wherein certain habits and norms and modes
of expression come to exert a kind of internal social control.
The result of this tendency over time is to create a cadre of
experts who are more interested in quoting and arguing with
one another than in considering the artistic works them-

[52] Ibid., 215.
[53] *Varied Types*, 252.

selves. Here is the source of the "staleness"[54] with which Chesterton charged the critics of his day.

According to Chesterton, the problem stems in part from the economics of the situation. Whether in academia or the popular media, there are always remunerations to consider. In a sense, said Chesterton, the critics are paid to tell lies:

> The critics and historians *were* paid to tell lies; though they may not have put the truth to themselves in quite so crude a fashion. They were academic officials of a certain academic system; achieving a fame which depended upon a fashion ... suiting themselves, consciously or unconsciously, to a certain school; and, when all is said, living by receiving salaries or selling books.[55]

The point here concerns not so much the lies as it does the tendency to suit oneself to a certain "school" of criticism and then to draw one's livelihood from success in promoting the prescribed opinions. Thus the critics become stale, as their criticisms follow a more predictable course as their careers progress.

As the critics labor to establish and defend the preferred giants among the artists, so there develops among the critics themselves a hierarchy of luminaries. Soon there are eminent personages whose opinions outweigh those of a dozen of the fainter stars, and eventually a quotation from a famous critic carries more weight than a direct observation from the original work of art itself. From the field of literature Chesterton drew this example:

> Only it seems funny to me that the critic should so solemnly make it a condemnation, in itself, of Mr. Dark's book on Stevenson, that it was not piously and reverently founded on

[54] *Glass Walking-Stick*, 167.
[55] *All Is Grist*, 182–83.

Mr. Swinnerton's book on Stevenson. For the critic, apparently Mr. Swinnerton is the one and only authority on Stevenson, and his sacred name must be invoked like that of a Muse
or a god of inspiration, at the beginning of any literary exercise on the subject.[56]

The famous critic has become the Muse, and all subsequent
critics are required to invoke his blessing.

While all of this nonsense may serve the peculiar economy of the critics and academics, it does very little to serve
the arts and the public. In Chesterton's view it all amounts
to a parasitic disease on the free expression of the imagination. "After all," he argued, "what we want is direct and
individual impressions of primary objects, whether poets or
pine-trees, and not an endless succession of critics learning
from critics how to criticize." [57]

In this chapter we have explored with G. K. Chesterton
the many forces and habits that work toward the extinction
of the imagination, particularly in the arts. There was the
broad reach of materialist philosophy, with its appeal to ob-
servable "realism" and its suppression of the spiritual and imaginative aspects of human life. There were those habits among
the artists and the "aesthetes", working to rob the arts of
their sense of wonder and, instead, seeking to calcify the arts
into the esoteric cult of a privileged class. Finally there were
the critics—with all their amoral relativism, their progressive
creed, their negativism and their critical fads—working to
mold the human imagination into fodder for their own hi-
erarchies of personal esteem.

It should be clear by now that the common denominator
of all of these phenomena is human pride. Materialism is the
proud philosophy grounded in the Enlightenment dream of

[56] *All I Survey*, 9.
[57] Ibid., 10.

humanity becoming its own god and seizing control of its own destiny. The obvious guiding principle in Chesterton's zoo of prigs, snobs, aesthetes, scholars, and critics is the standard human desire to be considered more important than other people. Here G. K. has given us a catalogue of the many ways that our personal pride works to distract, deflect, corrupt, co-opt, frustrate, and even destroy our God-given capacities for imagination.

In the end, pride is indeed the sickness, and humility is indeed the cure. With regard to the Christian imagination, it can be accurately said that the true Christian faith is the cure. For the pages of the Bible are full of the promise that if we humble ourselves before our God and our neighbor, we shall be free to enjoy the fruit of being a child of the Creator—a precious work of art made in the very image of the most glorious Artist of all.

Chapter Four

Songs, Poems, Stories, and Pictures

G. K. Chesterton was a man of many talents and of strong opinions. Among his opinions the reader can no doubt find ample materials for both agreement and disagreement—perhaps even an occasion to take offense. Among G. K.'s arts there was not only a broad spectrum of imaginative expressions but an admittedly wide variation in the quality of his talents as well. Though Chesterton's opinions were not always the best nor his artistic efforts always masterful, his works invariably stimulate the reader to greater heights of thinking and imagination. His arguments are full of the passion and color that define the man as an artist and a Christian believer.

The intention here is to take some time to revisit Chesterton's various artistic expressions in view of his stated opinions on the several genres in which he dabbled. Having already explored his general ideas on Christian imagination and the many forces that seek to extinguish its flame, now we look at Chesterton the artist and commentator in the areas of songs, poetry, stories, drama, essays, and drawing respectively. Again as before, though the way is strewn with argument and controversy, the journey should prove to be an enjoyable adventure nevertheless.

G. K. Chesterton was a lover of songs. Scattered among his poetry and fiction there are many songs that were obviously

83

written with the intention that they be put to music. In fact, the following lines from one of his poems stand as an open invitation to musicians:

> Words, for alas my trade is words,
>   a barren burst of rhymes,
> Rubbed by a hundred rhymsters,
>   battered a thousand times,
> Take them, you, that smile on strings,
>   those nobler sounds than mine,
> The words that never lie, or brag,
>   or flatter, or malign.[1]

One can hardly read Chesterton and not very soon come to realize the central importance of music in his thoughts on the life well lived.

Chesterton wrote a great many poems and songs, and he would most certainly point out that a songwriter is a poet in the noblest sense of the word. In fact, Chesterton argued that the writer of popular songs is something closer to a true poet than is the writer of obscure free verse that only a handful of specialists can understand. The best poetry, he believed, has much in common with the best songs, and much of what Chesterton had to say about one applies equally to the other.

We know, of course, that some of his lyrics were put to music and that the effect was marvelous—as in "A Christmas Carol" visited earlier. This carol is a tender ballad that is often heard among the traditional Christmas songs. The majority of Chesterton's songs, however, are far from tender and seem more at home in the mouths of the tavern crowd than of Christmas carolers. Most of Chesterton's songs were

---

[1] *The Collected Works of G. K. Chesterton*, vol. 10, pt. 1 (San Francisco: Ignatius Press, 1994), 333.

rowdy songs, drinking songs, and fighting songs. More times than not, they were songs of protest and revolution. Recall "The Song of Quoodle", which we saw earlier, wherein Chesterton protested the materialist world view and the arrogance of empirical scientism. Other protest songs were "The Song against Grocers", lamenting the decline of common dining and fellowship in the old English inns;[2] a song called "History", opposing the seizure of English public lands by the rich;[3] and another called "For the Creche", sung against the induction of mothers into the industrial work force. A stanza from this latter song bears repeating:

> For mother is happy in greasing a wheel
> For somebody else, who is cornering Steel;
> And though our one meeting was not very long,
> She took the occasion to sing me this song:
> 'O, hush thee, my baby, the time will soon come
> When thy sleep will be broken with hooting and hum;
> There are handles want turning and turning all day,
> And knobs to be pressed in the usual way;
>
> O, hush thee, my baby, take rest while I croon,
> For Progress comes early, and Freedom too soon.'[4]

In the name of Progress and Freedom for women, the Industrial Revolution deprived millions of babies of their mothers. Chesterton's song from a baby's point of view puts a sting into the words "progress" and "freedom", which had gained such widespread applause. There are many other Chesterton songs to be found, mostly in the books *Greybeards at Play*; *Wine, Water and Song*; *The Flying Inn*; and *The Works of G. K. Chesterton.*

[2] G. K. Chesterton, *Greybeards at Play* (London: Elek, 1974), 72.
[3] Ibid., 80.
[4] Ibid., 83–84.

Besides writing songs himself, Chesterton had a great deal to say *about* songs. For several reasons he liked many of the older styles better than the new. For one reason, he felt that the old songs had a kind of gusto that had faded somewhat in the modern songs. In comparing medieval hymns with modern ones, he wrote:

> There is a quality in these medieval songs that can only be expressed by the medieval word "lusty." There is a grand and even gigantic gusto, which is never found in modern moral and religious poetry. . . . The good news seems to be not only really good but really new. It is hailed with a sort of shout. . . . I will not attempt to inquire here why the medieval carol, as distinct from the modern hymn, could manage to achieve the resounding quality of that shout. I should be inclined to suggest that some part of it may have been due to men really believing that there was something to shout about.[5]

Chesterton was talking about the kind of gusto that comes from a person who really believes that there is something worth shouting about. Chesterton himself felt that kind of passion about the terrible effects of the urban-industrial economy upon the common English people, and his shouting came through in the lines of his songs. For example, in a song called "History", he wrote:

> The people they left the land, the land
> But they went on working hard;
> And the village green that got mislaid
> Turned up in the squire's back-yard:
> But twenty men of us all got work
> On a bit of his motor car;
> And we all became, with the world's acclaim,
> The marvellous mugs we are.[6]

[5] G. K. Chesterton, *Generally Speaking* (New York: Dodd, Mead and Company, 1929), 200–201.
[6] *Greybeards at Play*, 82.

There was just this sort of rough-and-tumble mixture of satire and gaiety in most of Chesterton's songs, reflecting his
passionate and unyielding—and, as a matter of fact, entirely
Christian—concern for the underdog. In his book *Heretics*,
he discussed how the old ballads served as his model:

> The rude old ballads are as sentimentally concerned for the
> under-dog as the Aborigines' Protection Society. When men
> were tough and raw, when they lived amid hard knocks and
> hard laws, when they knew what fighting really was, they
> had only two kinds of songs. The first was a rejoicing that
> the weak had conquered the strong, the second a lamenta-
> tion that the strong had, for once in a way, conquered the
> weak. For this defiance of the *status quo* ... this premature
> challenge to the powerful, is the whole nature and inmost
> secret of the psychological adventure which is called man.[7]

In another context, G. K. expressed his respect for those "old
and pompous patriotic songs"[8] and elsewhere his love for
the older Christmas carols, both for their dignity and style—as
he put it, "a certain natural carriage and distinction of diction: what we have come to call style".[9] Here is his basis for
the idea that a good songwriter is indeed a poet, because a
good song calls for an artful coordination of substance and style.

Speaking of style in songs and poetry, Chesterton always
defended the use of both rhythm and rhyme. He claimed
that nothing is more natural than "the sort of melody that
makes the beauty of any old song."[10] In this regard he once
argued:

[7] G. K. Chesterton, *Heretics*, in *The Collected Works of G. K. Chesterton*, vol. 1
(San Francisco: Ignatius Press, 1986), 83.

[8] G. K. Chesterton, *Autobiography*, *The Collected Works of G. K. Chesterton*,
vol. 16 (San Francisco: Ignatius Press, 1988), 23.

[9] *Generally Speaking*, 194.

[10] G. K. Chesterton, *Fancies versus Fads* (London: Methuen and Company,
1923), 5.

I have always had the fancy that if a man were really free, he would talk in rhythm and even in rhyme. His most hurried post-card would be a sonnet; and his most hasty wires like harp-strings. He would breathe a song into the telephone; a song which would be a lyric or an epic, according to the time involved in awaiting the call; or in his inevitable altercation with the telephone girl, the duel would be also a duet. He would express his preference among the dishes at dinner in short impromptu poems, combining the more mystical gratitude of grace with a certain epigrammatic terseness, more convenient for domestic good feeling.[11]

It is the free soul that is always ready to break into rhythm and rhyme; the modern disdain for such things constitutes a new kind of bondage.

According to Chesterton, songs can be the most powerful among the modes of imaginative expression, because they naturally synthesize sound and meaning. While Enlightenment thinking tends to separate sound and meaning into such pseudo-scientific categories as "phonetics" and "semantics", Chesterton insisted that in song they become inseparable. The sound has its own meaning, and in a well-written song the sounds and the ideas combine to create the meaning. In this connection, Chesterton wrote:

The only thing I am quite sure about is that the sense depends on the sound and the sound depends on the sense. It actually would not sound the same, if another meaning were expressed by the same sound. It actually would not mean as much, if other words expressed the same meaning.[12]

Chesterton flatly rejected the simple psychological explanation of this phenomenon. He was not talking about a kind

[11] Ibid., 76–77.
[12] G. K. Chesterton, *All I Survey* (New York: Books for Libraries Press, 1967), 102.

of mental association with past events, but a response that is intrinsic to the sound itself. He explained:

> Certainly three notes on a piano can bring tears to the eyes by reminding us of a dead friend; though certainly the first noise is not the noise he made when whistling to his dog, nor the second the noise he made when kicking his boots off, nor the third the noise he made when blowing his nose.[13]

The sound itself has its own meaning, and the true artistry of the songwriter involves bringing together the perfect tunes with the perfect words.

Such perfection is indeed a tall order, and yet it happens. We can feel it when it happens. There are certain lines in certain songs that simply get into us and resonate and take hold of us, and in these lines the writer has found that perfect synthesis. Chesterton claimed that "it is not enough that the musician should get his music out of him. It is also his business to get his music into somebody else." [14] G. K. felt that music is one of those miraculous human endowments that reflect something of the Creator, and as such, song becomes a medium by which we touch the very bedrock of our humanity.

Finally, it was very important to Chesterton that songs be songs for the people. He blamed scientism for taking songs from the people and reserving them for specialists. In *Heretics*, he wrote:

> But if we look at the progress of our scientific civilization we see a gradual increase everywhere of the specialist over the popular function. Once men sang together round a table in chorus; now one man sings alone, for the absurd reason that

[13] G. K. Chesterton, *The Uses of Diversity* (New York: Dodd, Mead and Company, 1921), 121.

[14] G. K. Chesterton, *The Glass Walking-Stick* (London: Methuen and Company, 1955), 183.

he can sing better. If scientific civilization goes on (which is
most improbable) only one man will laugh, because he can
laugh better than the rest.[15]

There is something good, Chesterton insisted, even some-
thing divinely approved in people joining together in song.
This glorious image of communal celebration permeates
G. K.'s own songs, as shown in such lines as:

> And we all became, with the world's acclaim,
> The marvellous mugs we are.[16]

Chesterton's lamenting and protest against the loss of communal singing is found most fully developed in his novel *The
Flying Inn*.

In earlier times, said Chesterton, when people were still
allowed to believe in the divine nature of music, the song
commanded the frivolous reverence it deserves. "In the old
religions of the world, indeed," he wrote, "people did think
the stars were dancing to the tunes of their temples; and they
danced as no man has danced since." [17] His point is certainly
not that we ought to imagine nature dancing to our tunes—
that would be something very close to Enlightenment
thinking—but that when people realize the divine connection in music, their songs and dances necessarily take on a
wonderful new dimension of celebration and praise.

In his zeal to give music its rightful place of honor in human society, Chesterton managed to offend a great many
people by an offhand remark in one of his newspaper essays.
There he complained of the habit of playing music at meals.
As a great eater and talker himself, he was naturally annoyed
that the music often caused the diners to resort to shouting

---

[15] *Heretics*, 164.

[16] *Greybeards at Play*, 82.

[17] G. K. Chesterton, *The Common Man* (New York: Sheed and Ward, 1950),
137.

to make themselves heard. Understandably, many of his readers wrote to tell him that they would rather hear music when
they ate than to listen to people like Chesterton and his friend
Belloc pontificating on economics and philosophy. In a subsequent article, Chesterton defended himself thus:

> I did not confine myself to complaining of meals being spoilt
> by music. I also complained of music being spoilt by meals.
> I was so impertinent as to suggest that if we want to listen to
> good music we should listen to it, and honour it with our
> undivided attention.[18]

Though tempted under the circumstances to doubt the sincerity of such a defense, we must recognize that it is probably true in Chesterton's case, because he was, indeed, a great
lover of good music and song.

What Chesterton felt about music he felt at least as deeply
about poetry, and much of his commentary on poetry is therefore fully germane to the writing of songs as well. That
Chesterton thought very highly of poets is attested in the
fact that most of the protagonists in his novels were poets
and painters—for example, Gabriel Syme in *The Man Who
Was Thursday*, Patrick Dalroy in *The Flying Inn*, and Gabriel
Gale in *The Poet and the Lunatics*. This preference for poets is
hardly surprising when one considers that the underlying
theme of so much of Chesterton's work was an assertion of
the Romantic view of humanity in the face of the popular
Enlightenment view. In a world already comatose from the
deadening effects of scientism, G. K. claimed a greater need
for poets and artists than ever before. "What are poets for,"
he asked, "except to go about asking everybody whether
they wake or sleep?"[19]

---

[18] *Generally Speaking*, 104.
[19] G. K. Chesterton, *Come to Think of It* (London: Methuen and Company, 1930), 21.

Chesterton never ventured a technical definition of poetry, but he made many passing comments revealing what he thought poetry ought to be. In *What I Saw in America*, he wrote "that poetry is emotion remembered in tranquillity; which may be extended to mean affection remembered in loneliness".[20] In another context he wrote:"It is often said that the office of Poet Laureate is not fitted to our times. This is true; it is perhaps the most compact condemnation of our times."[21] Our times are the times of scientism—the times when imagination and feeling are devalued in favor of something called "hard facts".

Here is the sense in which Chesterton considered the poet to be a revolutionary. If the established order is all about empirical observations and numbers, the revolutionary is he who dares to oppose that order. "In every man's heart there is a revolution"; he once wrote, "how much more in every poet's?"[22] A revolution, however, is not the same thing as anarchy; the true revolutionary builds something better. Speaking of revolutionary poetry, Chesterton observed:

> There seems to be a crazy tradition from the Byronic or Bohemian culture, that poetry must be revolutionary in the sense of destructive. It would seem obvious that poetry can only be creative. But poetry can also be, in a way of its own, constructive.... The poet is by derivation the Maker, and wishes, not only to imagine but to make.[23]

Along this same line Gabriel Syme in *The Man Who Was Thursday* argues: "[W]hat is there poetical about being in revolt? You might as well say that it is poetical to be sea-sick.

<hr>

[20] G. K. Chesterton, *What I Saw in America*, in *The Collected Works of G. K. Chesterton*, vol. 21 (San Francisco: Ignatius Press, 1990), 250.

[21] G. K. Chesterton, *All Is Grist* (New York: Books for Libraries Press, 1967), 164.

[22] G. K. Chesterton, *Varied Types* (New York: Dodd, Mead and Company, 1903), 251.

[23] *Glass Walking-Stick*, 180.

Being sick is a revolt." [24] And in yet another context, Chesterton makes the rather paradoxical claim that "all the poetry that professed to be particularly revolutionary was in fact particularly traditional." [25]

Here is another major theme that runs through all of Chesterton's work. The very purpose of his nonfiction masterpiece *Orthodoxy* is to point out how very revolutionary is traditional Christian doctrine in a world that has for more than a century sworn complete allegiance to the doctrines of scientism. The basic point of Chesterton's distributist economics was a revolutionary effort to restore a traditional emphasis on free individuals having good jobs and homes of their own. In the arts, as we have seen here, the same theme emerges in Chesterton's insistence that the progressive clamor against form, beauty, valuation, and meaning compels him to look back toward more traditional forms and ideas. The idea is captured well in the phrase "a toppling construction" as applied to the activities of Innocent Smith in the novel *Manalive*.[26] It is accurate to say that Chesterton considered a toppling construction to be the proper work of every poet, and even more certainly every Christian poet.

This idea of a toppling construction suggests several implications, one of which is a rejection of mere pessimism or negativism in the arts. Anyone, G. K. observed, can tear things down; it takes no special genius to expose the follies and evils of contemporary life. Real genius is a positive source of ideas. In *The Common Man*, Chesterton wrote about:

> what alone can make a literary man great. It is ideas; the power of generating and making vivid an incessant output of

[24] G. K. Chesterton, *The Man Who Was Thursday*, in *The Collected Works of G. K. Chesterton*, vol. 6 (San Francisco: Ignatius Press, 1991), 479.

[25] *Come to Think of It*, 44.

[26] G. K. Chesterton, *Manalive* (London: Thomas Nelson and Sons, 1915), 60.

ideas. It is untrue to say that what matters is quality and not quantity.... Many forgotten poets have let fall a lyric with one really perfect image: but when we open any play of Shakespeare, good or bad, at any page, important or un-important, with the practical certainty of finding some imagery that at least arrests the eye and probably enriches the memory, we are putting our trust in a great man.[27]

It is the incessant output of positive ideas that defines the great poet and artist. If all of one's poetry consists simply in exposing and complaining about things, then Chesterton would say that one is not a poet at all.

A good illustration of Chesterton's attitude here is found in his essay on the early pessimistic poems of T. S. Eliot, particularly "The Waste Land" and "The Hollow Men". While Chesterton concedes that there is some truth in Eliot's images of the heartless and headless people of our age, he refuses to concede any inevitability in the matter. For the living and fighting Christian, at any rate, the end is not "the supplication of a dead man's hand under a fading star" but a triumph of resurrection to the glory beyond the sky. In his book *The Spice of Life*, Chesterton reacted to Eliot's famous lines in "The Hollow Men", which say:

> This is the way the world ends
> Not with a bang but a whimper

Here is Chesterton's reply:

> Now forgive me if I say, in my old-world fashion, that I'm damned if I ever felt like that. I recognize the great realities Mr. Eliot has revealed; but I do not admit that this is the deepest reality.... It is doubtless a grotesque spectacle that the great-grandfathers should still be dancing with indecent gaiety, when the young are so grave and sad; but in this mat-

[27] *Common Man*, 144–45.

ter of the spice of life, I will defend the spiritual appetite of my own age. I will even be so indecently frivolous as to break into song, and say to the young pessimists:—

> Some sneer; some snigger; some simper;
> In the youth where we laughed and sang,
> And *they* may end with a whimper
> But *we* will end with a bang.[28]

Yet another issue of great importance to Chesterton was the relation between poetry and reality. Again, the doctrines of scientism set practical reality on one side and poetry on the opposite side. In this connection Chesterton wrote of a certain man:

> He is a poet; therefore a practical man. The affinity of the two words ... is much nearer than many people suppose, for the matter of that. There is one Greek word for "I do" from which we get the word practical, and another Greek word for "I do" from which we get the word poet.... The two words practical and poetical may mean two subtly different things in that old and subtle language, but they mean the same in English and the same in the long run. It is ridiculous to suppose that the man who can understand the inmost intricacies of a human being who has never existed at all cannot make a guess at the conduct of the man who lives next door.... It is idle, in short, for a man who has created men to say that he does not understand them.[29]

In another place Chesterton mentions that "poetry is so much nearer to reality than all other human occupations." [30] Thus, Chesterton was not one to concede to scientism any kind of superior ability to distinguish truth from untruth, as he held

[28] G. K. Chesterton, *The Spice of Life* (Beaconsfield, Eng.: D. Finlayson, 1964), 167.
[29] *Varied Types*, 238–39.
[30] Ibid., 240.

that the rational-empirical method was entirely inadequate for the understanding of humanity or God.

There were countless others, however, who accepted even the wildest claims of scientism and proceeded to use its tenets as a test of truth in every field of knowledge—from physics to biology to psychology to theology. Even the arts were not spared from the cult of scientism, as illustrated, for example, in the field of literature as the flood of the new Realism pushed the older Romanticism out of its way. In the face of all this scientistic enthusiasm, Chesterton wondered what poetic heights might have been reached if the Copernican view had not sacrificed the imagination in the pursuit of objectivity. In *The Defendant*, Chesterton wrote, not without a touch of sarcasm:

> It would be an interesting speculation to imagine whether the world will ever develop a Copernican poetry and a Copernican habit of fancy; whether we shall ever speak of "early earth-turn" instead of "early sunrise," and speak indifferently of looking up at the daisies, or looking down on the stars. But if we ever do, there are really a large number of big and fantastic facts awaiting us, worthy to make a new mythology.... If we once realise all this earth as it is, we should find ourselves in a land of miracles: we shall discover a new planet at the moment that we discover our own. Among all these strange things that men have forgotten, the most universal and catastrophic lapse of memory is that by which they have forgotten that they are living on a star.... But for some mysterious reason this habit of realising poetically the facts of science has ceased abruptly with scientific progress, and all the confounding portents preached by Galileo and Newton have fallen on deaf ears. They painted a picture of the universe compared with which the Apocalypse with its falling stars was a mere idyll. They declared that we are all careening through space, clinging to a cannon-ball, and the poets ignore the matter as if it were a remark about the

weather. They say that an invisible force holds us in our own arm-chairs while the earth hurtles like a boomerang; and men still go back to dusty records to prove the mercy of God.... To what towering heights of poetic imagery might we not have risen if only the poetising of natural history had continued and man's fancy had played with the planets as naturally as it once played with the flowers![31]

Here again Chesterton returned to the definition of a poet and the function of imagination. We come to see what he means about the revolutionary imagination when he says that "the function of imagination is not to make strange things settled, so much as to make settled things strange; not so much to make wonders facts as to make facts wonders."[32]

Besides defending the realism of poetry, Chesterton also spoke of the democratic nature of poetry. Rejecting the snobbish idea that poetry is a specialized form of art for the exclusive enjoyment of the erudite few, Chesterton felt that the best poetry expresses the common feelings of humanity. In this regard he wrote:

It is no valid accusation against a poet that the sentiment he expresses is commonplace. Poetry is always commonplace; it is vulgar in the noblest sense of that noble word.... Unless he is to some extent a demagogue, he cannot be a poet.[33]

To this sentiment Chesterton later added that "poetry, like religion, is always a democratic thing, even if it pretends the contrary."[34] Using Rudyard Kipling as an example,

[31] G. K. Chesterton, *The Defendant* (London: J. M. Dent and Sons, 1907), 77–79.
[32] Ibid., 84.
[33] *Varied Types*, 250.
[34] Ibid., 251.

Chesterton exposed one of the intrinsic conflicts in a poet's mind. He wrote:

> He desires to be the poet of his people, bone of their bone, and flesh of their flesh, understanding their origins, celebrating their destiny.... Having been given by the gods originality—that is, disagreement with others—he desires divinely to agree with them.[35]

We saw earlier how Chesterton felt that all of the arts are, at their most basic level, an attempt to communicate with one's fellows in society.

In the same manner as in his discussions of songs, Chesterton remained a strong advocate of rhythm and repetition in poetry as well. It must be understood here that by Chesterton's time, the trends in modern poetry were already well established in the abandonment of both rhyme and meter. Thus again, Chesterton put himself in a position very familiar to the Christian believer—that is, being a revolutionary advocate of a traditional cause. In this case Chesterton argued passionately for the value of repetition in poetry. In *Orthodoxy*, he again appealed to the child:

> A child kicks his legs rhythmically through excess, not absence, of life. Because children have abounding vitality, because they are in spirit fierce and free, therefore they want things repeated and unchanged. They always say, "Do it again"; and the grown-up person does it again until he is nearly dead.[36]

It was not only repetition, however, that Chesterton defended but the presence of rhythm or a regular meter as well.

[35] *Heretics*, 198.
[36] G. K. Chesterton, *Orthodoxy*, in *The Collected Works of G. K. Chesterton*, vol. 1 (San Francisco: Ignatius Press, 1986), 263.

In *All I Survey*, Chesterton explained his position at some length:

> I think there are much deeper difficulties than are now gen-
> erally understood about breaking with the traditions of
> rhythm. I do not say it should not be done, but I do say that
> it is doubtful whether those who do it know what they are
> doing ... the old conventions of verse rested upon instincts
> which are perhaps indestructible, but which at least cannot
> be casually destroyed.... But something much deeper and
> more mysterious is involved. The old poets had a power of
> mixing with their fleecy clouds and hairy comets some an-
> cestral magic of the nature of music ... weighted with har-
> monies and a historic richness that prevented them from being
> crude, even when they were new. It seems to me that the
> new poets do not try to recover that ancient wedding of
> sound and sense ... even the best of them seem to be seek-
> ing a divorce rather than a wedding.[37]

The contemporary habit of sneering at poetry with rhythm
and rhyme is nothing more, said Chesterton, than an arbitrary fad that actually impoverishes poetic expression.

In his defense of rhythm in poetry, G. K. argued that "metre is not artificial but elemental; it is smooth like Niagara.
Metre is more natural than free verse; because it has more of
the movement of nature, and the curves of wind and wave."[38]
In another slightly sarcastic comparison, Chesterton compared the traditional poetry of Alexander Pope with a modern poet:

> Instead of writing "A being darkly wise and rudely great," a
> contemporary poet, in his elaborately ornamental book of
> verses, would produce something like the following:—

[37] *All I Survey*, 104–6.
[38] *Common Man*, 215.

> "A creature
> Of feature
> More dark, more dark, more dark than
>   skies,
> Yea, darkly wise, yea, darkly wise:
> Darkly wise as a formless fate ..." etc.[39]

And in a discussion on Walt Whitman, Chesterton argued:

> He was mistaken in abandoning metre in poetry.... In for-
> saking metre he was forsaking something quite wild and bar-
> barous, something as instinctive as anger and as necessary as
> meat. He forgot that all real things move in a rhythm, that
> the heart beats in harmony, and the seas rise and ebb in har-
> mony.... The whole world talks poetry; it is only we who,
> with elaborate ingenuity, manage to talk prose.[40]

Here is certainly a consistent Chestertonian theme. Though
God created nature full of poetic rhythm, we have managed
to blind and deafen ourselves to the point where it no longer
seems natural. The consequence now is that our choppy and
disjointed language merely reflects our confused and alien-
ated existence.

Again in poetry as much as in song, sound and sense prop-
erly work together to produce the perfect poem. Yet the
poetic fad has moved entirely away from the control of sound.
Chesterton stated the case this way: "In plain words, imaginative poetry must not appeal to the sense of sound. The
futurist poet is like the Early Victorian child. He must be
seen and not heard."[41] Speaking of sound and sense in poetry, G. K. reiterated that "the two things bring each other

---

[39] G. K. Chesterton, *Five Types* (New York: Books for Libraries Press, 1969),
17–18.

[40] G. K. Chesterton, *Lunacy and Letters* (New York: Sheed and Ward, 1958),
64.

[41] *Come to Think of It*, 34.

out, as certain condiments are said to bring out certain flavours." [42] Having read a review in which the critic complained of a poem seeming too melodic, Chesterton reacted thus:

> Crimes of this sort our critics seem more and more bent on bringing to light; but the code of law which they administer ... appears sometimes to be a little vague. It is not easy for the outsider to understand why words that might be inspiring and imaginative if only they were cacophonous and clumsy can become less intelligent or suggestive merely by being sonorous or sweet. But there seems really to be an idea, in some of the critics, that the poet should avoid pleasing the ear, quite apart from his duty to please the mind. [43]

Though Chesterton's opinions may seem to some to be intellectually out-of-date, it remains difficult to justify the widespread sneering at poems with rhyme and meter.

The use of rhyme in poetry has now been so thoroughly rejected that it is considered appropriate only for small children. Yet here lies the connection that Chesterton seized as an argument in favor of rhyming. "Poets must put away childish things," G. K. observed, "including the child's pleasure in the mere sing-song of irrational rhyme. It may be hinted that when poets put away childish things they may put away poetry." [44] In another context Chesterton expanded on this thought:

> But rhyme has a supreme appropriateness for the treatment of the higher comedy.... It is far more conceivable that men's speech should flower naturally into these harmonious forms, when they are filled with the essential spirit of youth, than when they are sitting gloomily in the presence of immemorial

[42] Ibid., 37–38.
[43] Ibid., 34.
[44] *Fancies versus Fads*, 5.

destiny. The great error consists in supposing that poetry is
an unnatural form of language. We should all like to speak
poetry at the moment when we truly live, and if we do not
speak it, it is because we have an impediment in our speech.
It is not song that is the narrow or artificial thing, it is conversation that is a broken and stammering attempt at song.. . .
Rhymes answer each other as the sexes in flowers and in
humanity answer each other.[45]

There is something in rhyme, said Chesterton, that we
find intrinsically and deeply satisfying—that is, unless we are
among those prigs who have taught themselves instead to
sneer. There is something in rhyme that appeals to our childlike sense of harmony, but there is also more than that. Chesterton wrote, "Rhyme gives a ringing finality to a statement;
the ear hears that something has been decided even before
the brain can take it in." [46] The point again is that the sound
and the sense become an artistic whole, and there is something less meaningful and less satisfying when sound is no
longer an important part of the expression.

Finally, speaking again of the poet in particular and of artists in general, Chesterton related these opinions to art, life,
and reality itself. In *Lunacy and Letters*, he wrote:

We talk of art as something artificial in comparison with life.
But I sometimes fancy that the very highest art is more real
than life itself. At least this is true: that in proportion as passions become real they become poetical; the lover is always
trying to be the poet. All real energy is an attempt at harmony and a high swing of rhythm; and if we were only real
enough we should all talk in rhyme.[47]

[45] *Five Types*, 50–51.
[46] *Lunacy and Letters*, 83.
[47] Ibid., 144.

Here is some truly revolutionary talk. Contemporary wisdom speaks of the artificial constraints in the old poetic forms, but Chesterton's toppling construction turns that popular notion on its head. Nothing could be more natural than rhythm and rhyme in language, he says, and nothing gets to the heart of reality better than good poetry. It is the very prosaic and stilted scholarly diction and trendy techno-babble that are the more likely paths to unreality.

Besides writing songs and poetry, Chesterton was prolific in the art of storytelling. Recall that it was his Father Brown mysteries that brought G. K. his first fame. The Father Brown mysteries can still be found in several large volumes, as they attract a worldwide readership even today. Some of Chesterton's novel-length books are really a series of interlacing stories—most notably *The Paradoxes of Mr. Pond*, *The Club of Queer Trades*, and *The Poet and the Lunatics*. Others, like *The Napoleon of Notting Hill* and *Manalive*, follow a form more like a traditional novel.

Whether the form be stories or novels, there is something about fiction, said Chesterton, that meets a basic human need. G. K. put it this way:

> But human beings cannot be human without some field of fancy or imagination; some vague idea of the romance of life; and even some holiday of the mind in a romance that is a refuge from life.
>
> Every healthy person at some period must feed on fiction as well as fact; because fact is a thing which the world gives to him, whereas fiction is a thing which he gives to the world.[48]

A good story is like food, an essential nutrient that the author can give to the world.

[48] *Spice of Life*, 30-31.

There is not only that hunger in the public to have imaginative stories, there is a hunger in the author to tell the stories. Speaking from his own considerable experience, Chesterton explained:

> Nobody understands it who has not had what can only be called the ache of the artist to find some sense and some story in the beautiful things he sees; his hunger for secrets and his anger at any tower or tree escaping with its tale untold. He feels that nothing is perfect unless it is personal. Without that the blind unconscious beauty of the world stands in its garden like a headless statue.[49]

One gets the impression of a story aching inside the author's mind, awaiting the expression that will complete that headless statue.

Concerning his own novels, Chesterton was the first to admit that they were "not as good as a real novelist would have made them"[50] but that they were good ideas rather poorly done. His biggest problem, he knew, was a distinct lack of subtlety, as he could not resist the urge to let his philosophical ideas completely dominate his characters. In his attempts to explain himself in this matter, he once referred abstractly to "that weight and movement of words, in which style and distinction and philosophy and experience are one".[51] At another time he put the matter this way: "In short," he wrote, "I could not be a novelist; because I really like to see ideas or notions wrestling naked, as it were, and not dressed up in a masquerade as men and women."[52]

The accuracy of Chesterton's self-assessment here is obvious in his novels. There he makes the valiant attempt to

[49] G. K. Chesterton, *The Everlasting Man*, in *The Collected Works of G. K. Chesterton*, vol. 2 (San Francisco: Ignatius Press, 1986), 236.
[50] *Autobiography*, 276.
[51] *Come to Think of It*, 29.
[52] *Autobiography*, 277.

dress his ideas up as men and women, but in the end the ideas have much more substance than do the characters. As a consequence his novels generally lack the depth of characterization found in the great novels, and his plots tend toward the fantastic as he seeks primarily to represent his ideas clearly. Chesterton knew well that his novels were not of the caliber of those of Charles Dickens or Jane Austen, but this knowledge did not deter him from dabbling in the genre nevertheless.

Chesterton was serious about the great importance of storytelling. On this matter he once wrote:

> All this is the origin of the one distinctly human thing—the story. There can be as good science about a turnip as a man. There can be, properly considered, as good philosophy about a turnip as a man.... There can be, without any question at all, as good higher mathematics about a turnip as a man. But I do not think ... that there could be as good a novel written about a turnip as about a man.[53]

And then again Chesterton argued:

> The thing called Fiction, then, is the main fact of our human supremacy. If you want to know what is our human kinship with Nature, with the brutes, and with the stars, you can find cartloads of big philosophical volumes to show it you. You will find our kinship with Nature in books on geology and books on metaphysics. But if you want to find our isolation and divinity, you must pick up a penny novelette.[54]

Chesterton pointed out that God has, in fact, created millions of individual stories that have been acted out in individual

---

[53] "A Much Repeated Repetition", in *The Chesterton Review* 19, no. 2, (Saskatoon, Saskatchewan: G. K. Chesterton Society, 1993), 147.

[54] Ibid., 147.

human lives. When we humans in turn create stories, we exercise that creativity that is our birthright as creatures made in the image of God.

One of Chesterton's best novels was his first, *The Napoleon of Notting Hill*. In this futuristic story, G. K. cleverly imbedded his opinions and arguments about the British Empire and the Boer War—both to which he was strongly opposed. In the novel a young idealist named Adam Wayne declares himself the Napoleon of the Notting Hill district of London, and he manages to raise an army to defend that neighborhood from encroachment by the forces of big business. The characters in the story personify the idealist, the cynic, the politician, and the businessman, and the plot proceeds to play out the conflict of intentions among them.

As the story unfolds, the reader discovers Chesterton's political meanings in the novel. Adam Wayne and the people of Notting Hill represent the independence-minded supporters of the Boers in South Africa, while the opposition represents Cecil Rhodes and the empire-minded British politicians and businessmen. In his novel, Chesterton was saying that the Boers had every right to their independence and that the British had no business in building an empire. In the story Adam Wayne has won independence for Notting Hill, but the people want it to become an empire, ruling the other sections of the city. Adam Wayne replies:

> Is it altogether impossible to make a thing good without it immediately insisting on being wicked? The glory of Notting Hill in having achieved its independence, has been enough for me to dream of for many years, as I sat beside the fire. Is it really not enough for you ...? Notting Hill is a nation. Why should it condescend to be a mere Empire? ...

> Do you not see that it is the glory of our achievement that
> we have infected the other cities with the idealism of Not-
> ting Hill?[55]

Insert the word "England" wherever Wayne said "Notting
Hill", and there is Chesterton's political statement about the
British Empire and the Boer War. England, he argued, stands
for national independence; it is a betrayal for England to oppose the independence of such nations as South Africa and
Ireland. Here is an excellent example of how Chesterton
used his novels to argue his political, philosophical, and theological points.

In a facetious but pointed digression, Chesterton once addressed the growing problem of lawsuits against authors for
using people's names for villains in their novels. Chesterton's
obvious question was how can an author be expected to avoid
using *someone's* real name for disreputable characters without
resorting to nonsense names or numbers. In this regard he
wrote:

> I remember, in the course of the controversy, that I sug-
> gested that we should have to fall back on some alternative
> to names, such as numbers, in describing the ringing repar-
> tees leading up to the duel in which the subtle and crafty
> 7991 died upon the sword of the too-impetuous 3893; or
> the vows breathed by the passionate lips of 771 in the ear of
> 707.[56]

Chesterton was not one to let a legal absurdity go unnoticed.

Though Chesterton wrote about a dozen novels, his true
love lay in "those popular works of fiction which are the joy

[55] G. K. Chesterton, *The Napoleon of Notting Hill*, in *The Collected Works of
G. K. Chesterton*, vol. 6 (San Francisco: Ignatius Press, 1991), 363–64.
[56] *Autobiography*, 183.

of my existence",[57] that is, detective mystery stories. He truly loved to read and write murder mysteries, and the reading public of London and the world came to cherish his Father Brown stories. The genesis of the Father Brown mysteries is a fascinating story in itself, as it gives a glimpse into the creative process of Chesterton's imagination. G. K. was visiting his friend, a Roman Catholic priest named Father O'Connor, and the two men had a private conversation about a particular form of evil. Chesterton was astonished at the depth of the priest's understanding of evil and the criminal mind. During the same visit Chesterton overheard a pair of college students disparaging the cloistered naïveté of the clerical life, and he was struck with the great irony that his friend O'Connor obviously knew a great deal more about "real life" than did his young critics. In his *Autobiography*, Chesterton wrote:

> There sprang up in my mind the vague idea of making some artistic use of these comic and yet tragic cross-purposes; and constructing a comedy in which a priest should appear to know nothing and in fact know more about crime than the criminals.[58]

Thus was the character Father Brown born in Chesterton's imagination.

The greater point of the Father Brown stories, however, had much to do with philosophy and theology. For into his various police detectives and medical examiners Chesterton infused the perspective of scientism and the natural sciences model of humanity and human behavior. On the other hand, into Father Brown he infused that broader spiritual concern for the human soul that is consistent with Christianity. Though most of the Father Brown stories deliver more entertainment than philosophical debate, the theme that runs through

[57] *All Is Grist*, 105.
[58] *Autobiography*, 318.

them all is this competition between the two opposing doctrines of scientism and Christianity. In the end, of course, it
is Father Brown's deeper vision into the human soul that is
able to solve the mysteries. In a story called "The Blue Cross",
Father Brown himself explains, "Has it never struck you that
a man who does next to nothing but hear men's real sins is
not likely to be wholly unaware of human evil?" [59]

Chesterton's dear friend and perennial adversary George
Bernard Shaw for many years urged G. K. to try his hand at
writing drama, because it seemed to Shaw that Chesterton's
imagination would serve particularly well in that genre. After resisting for years, Chesterton finally in 1913 wrote *Magic*,
a respectable effort, especially for a first attempt. Over the
years he wrote only three other plays, and none of his drama
ever received critical acclaim.

Perhaps the most enjoyable of his dramas was *The Surprise*,
as Chesterton explored the Incarnation of Christ in a very
clever play within a play. Here is an engaging story about an
author who is not satisfied until his characters are in fact
given wills of their own. Once this has happened, the characters act out the pride, selfishness, and greed that are so
typical of human behavior. Predictably, the author becomes
very upset, and in the end he pokes his head through the sky
in the backdrop and exclaims, "What do you think you are
doing to my play? Drop it! Stop! I am coming down." [60] In
this way Chesterton sought to dramatize the relationships
among God's creation of human will, God's providence in
history, and God's incarnation as Jesus Christ.

Concerning drama Chesterton was passionate in his insistence that a play ought to be a treat to the audience. Reacting

---

[59] G. K. Chesterton, *The Complete Father Brown* (New York: Dodd, Mead
and Company, 1951), 23.

[60] G. K. Chesterton, *The Surprise* (New York: Sheed and Ward, 1953), 63.

against the contemporary fad of "slice-of-life realism" in drama, Chesterton wrote:

> If it is "like Life," if it represents the dull and throbbing routine of our actual life and exhibits only the emotions with which we commonly regard it ... it is not a play. That is the damning, but neglected error of so much modern realistic drama; the play fails to be a festival; and therefore fails to be a play.[61]

Chesterton felt that the playwright owes the audience a treat; not another hour or two of what is humdrum or ugly in everyday life. For this reason he felt that Ibsenism was destroying the theater. In this regard he wrote:

> For what is the theatre? First and last, and above all things, it is a festival.... The theatre is nothing if it is not joyful; and theatre is nothing if it is not sensational; the theatre is nothing if it is not theatrical. A play may be happy, it may be sad, it may be wild, it may be quiet, it may be tragic, it may be comic, but it must be festive.... It must, in modern phraseology, be a "treat."[62]

In drama, Chesterton said, the audience should have the final word. "There is a threadbare joke", he wrote, "which calls the gallery in a theatre 'the gods.' For my part I accept the joke quite seriously. The people in the galleries are ... the ultimate authority."[63] Chesterton's argument was that the gallery, the common people in the audience, do not come to a play hoping to see another slice of ordinary life; they come for a festival. As Chesterton dared to assert that there is nothing wrong with beauty in art, he also insisted that there is nothing wrong with festivity in drama. He wrote:

[61] *Lunacy and Letters*, 40.
[62] Ibid., 39–40.
[63] Ibid., 120.

... although two thousand years have beaten vainly upon the follies of the *Frogs* as on the wisdom of the *Republic*. It is all a mean shame of joy. When we come out from a performance of *Midsummer Night's Dream* we feel as near to the stars as when we come out from *King Lear*. For the joy of these works is older than sorrow, their extravagance is saner than wisdom, their love is stronger than death.[64]

Though the prigs and aesthetes may consider undiluted joy to be below their tastes, the classics prove the narrowness of the sophisticated view.

The issue here is bigger than drama or even the arts in general. Chesterton's concern reaches again into the depths of human experience and the forces that work to extinguish our God-given capacities for joy. He wrote:

The old masters of a healthy madness, Aristophanes or Rabelais or Shakespeare, doubtless had many brushes with the precisians or aesthetics of their day, but we cannot but feel that for honest severity and consistent self-maceration they would always have had respect. But what abysses of scorn, inconceivable to any modern, would they have reserved for an aesthetic type and movement which violated morality and did not even find pleasure, which outraged sanity and could not attain to exuberance, which contented itself with the fool's cap without the bells![65]

What would Shakespeare and company have said about the modern arts which so self-consciously violate morality and then so self-importantly avoid pleasure? Chesterton uses the phrase "abysses of scorn" to express his answer. It is not, he said, a legitimate use of the arts to make people either bad or unhappy.

[64] *Defendant*, 127.
[65] Ibid.

Now to look only briefly at the art of writing essays, Chesterton seems paradoxical in his comments and his actions. As a matter of fact, he loved to write essays, and he made his living at writing them for the newspapers and journals; as a matter of opinion he considered essays to be among the most dangerous forms of communication. In *The Glass Walking-Stick*, he wrote:

> There are dark and morbid moods in which I am tempted to feel that Evil re-entered the world in the form of Essays. The Essay is like the Serpent, smooth and graceful and easy of movement, also wavering and wandering. Besides, I suppose that the very word Essay had the original meaning of "trying it on." The serpent was in every sense of the word tentative. The tempter is always feeling his way, and finding out how much other people will stand. That misleading air of irresponsibility about the Essay is very disarming though appearing to be disarmed.[66]

The problem in Chesterton's eyes is a matter of accountability, that the essayist can easily escape being held to a standard. G. K. added:

> There is really an element in modern letters which is at once indefinite and dangerous.... By its very nature it does not exactly explain what it is trying to do and thus escapes a decisive judgement about whether it has really done it.[67]

To such irresponsibility Chesterton objected on artistic grounds and with regard to the honest exchange of ideas.

Again Chesterton pointed to the past for a better model, thus flying in the face of the presentism in popular progressive thought. Comparing the medieval mind with the modern, he wrote:

[66] *Glass Walking-Stick*, 186.
[67] Ibid., 187.

The medieval man thought in terms of a Thesis, where the modern man thinks in terms of the Essay. It would be unfair, perhaps, to say that the modern man only essays to think— or, in other words, makes a desperate attempt to think. But it would be true to say that the modern man often only essays, or attempts, to come to a conclusion. Whereas the medieval man hardly thought it worthwhile to think at all, unless he could come to a conclusion.[68]

Though the modern essayist feels free to wander at will, Chesterton felt that the reader wants closure. "After a certain amount of wandering," he concluded, "the mind wants either to get there or to go home."[69]

Despite his own very real objections to those vague and wandering essays, Chesterton made some of his most important intellectual and moral contributions in his essays. Though he criticized the essay form on the grounds of accountability, G. K. himself was far from irresponsible in his essays. Most of his essays came to a very definite conclusion, and—though his style was often humorous—their point was generally a matter of considerable depth and consequence. In his weekly journalism, Chesterton served the essential function of taking to the public forum the reasonable presentation and defense of a Christian view of the world and contemporary events. For this reason Chesterton's collections of essays continue to inform and convince even as they entertain.

There are two things, however, that make Chesterton's essays decisively more enjoyable to read than most others. For one, most writers of essays tend to take themselves very seriously, but in Chesterton's essays there is always that undercurrent of the tongue in the cheek—a kind of farcical attitude revealing a man ready to laugh also at himself. For

[68] Ibid., 187–88.
[69] Ibid., 189.

another, Chesterton's prose very often reads like poetry. For this reason there is never a dull moment in Chesterton's essays. For example, in an essay called "The Garden of the Sea", Chesterton gave this passing illustration:

> Consider, for instance, what wastes of wordy imitation and ambiguity the ordinary educated person in the big towns could pour out on the subject of the sea. A country girl I know in the county of Buckingham had never seen the sea in her life until the other day. When she was asked what she thought of it she said it was like cauliflowers. Now that is a piece of pure literature—vivid, entirely independent and original, and perfectly true. I always had been haunted with an analogous kinship which I could never locate; cabbages always remind me of the sea and the sea always reminds me of cabbages. It is partly, perhaps, the veined mingling of violet and green, as in the sea a purple that is almost dark red may mix with a green that is almost yellow, and still be the blue sea as a whole.... But just where my fancy halted the Buckinghamshire young woman rushed (so to speak) to my imaginative rescue. Cauliflowers are twenty times better than cabbages, for they show the waves breaking as well as curling, and the efflorescence of the branching foam, blind bubbling, and opaque. Moreover, the strong lines of life are suggested; the arches of the rushing waves have all the rigid energy of green stalks, as if the whole sea were one great green plant with one immense white flower rooted in the abyss.[70]

Some of Chesterton's most accessible and delightful writing appears in his essays, and there are many collections of his essays among which readers can choose freely.

Finally, there are the visual arts and Chesterton's lifelong love of drawing. The previous excerpt from "The Garden of

[70] G. K. Chesterton, *Alarms and Discursions* (London: Methuen and Company, 1927), 208–9.

the Sea" reveals a fascination with colors that truly typifies Chesterton as an artist and author. Most of his fiction and much of his nonfiction writing contains such descriptive passages that vividly depict colors and shapes. Another example is a comment in his *Autobiography* remembering his childhood: "But when I remember that these forgotten crayons contained a stick of 'light red,' seemingly a more commonplace colour, the point of that dull red pencil pricks me as if it could draw red blood." [71] Another example is found in *Lunacy and Letters*:

> But let us remember that wherever the crimson of a sunset cloud meets the violet of a distant hill it is by honest artistic canons equally discordant and offensive. The purest heavens, the most silver clouds, the most verdant meadows may combine in a riot of incongruity such as was never seen on the bonnet of a flower-girl. [72]

Some may find it surprising to learn that Chesterton considered drawing to be an act of courage. In *The Common Man*, he explained:

> The art of drawing, for example, requires even a kind of physical courage. Any one who has tried to draw a straight line and failed knows that he failed chiefly in nerve, as he might fail to jump off a cliff. [73]

At their best the arts consist of positive expressions by the artist, and Chesterton emphasized the courage required for making such an expression for all to see and judge. Again we can recall the relatively risk-free aspect of so much negative criticism as contrasted with the intrinsic vulnerability of the creative artist.

[71] *Autobiography*, 45.
[72] *Lunacy and Letters*, 20.
[73] *Common Man*, 186.

There is also the matter of art as a departure from nature. If Chesterton was correct in his belief that art-making defines humans as the prodigy in nature, our artistic efforts become radical statements in defiance of the deterministic view of evolution. In this regard he wrote:

> For it is the whole business of humanity in this world to deny evolution, to make absolute distinctions, to take a pen and draw round certain actions a line that nature does not recognize; to take a pencil and draw round the human face a black line that is not there.[74]

What is Chesterton getting at here? He is reacting against the broad evolutionary, progressive, relativist blurring of distinctions where there are truly important distinctions to be made. It is essential to assert that it is humanity—and not apes or monkeys—that needs to draw lines around things. Thus, Chesterton calls upon humans to be humans boldly—to resist the corrosive influence of evolutionary relativism and instead actually to glory in the distinctions.

No one should be surprised, then, to learn that Chesterton deplored impressionism and preferred the robust paintings of the Florentines. In this regard he wrote:

> If these old artists draw a ship, everything is sacrificed to expressing the "shippishness" of the ship. If they draw a tower, its whole object is to be towering. If they draw a flower, its whole object is to be flowering.[75]

In another context, Chesterton expanded this thought:

> The modern artist may have his own reasons for drawing legs as if they were bolsters or sausages; but that does not make the strong sweeping lines, of sloping bone or gripping muscle, in a great Florentine drawing, a dull mechanical re-

[74] *Lunacy and Letters*, 79.
[75] Ibid., 113.

production, valuable only as a vulgar snapshot of trivial fact. Those lines are strong and beautiful, as the lines of a waterfall and whirlpool are beautiful. In fact, they are exactly like the beautiful abstract forms, which the modern artist would like to invent—if he could.[76]

Elsewhere he wrote, "Rembrandt declared that sane and manly gospel that a man was dignified, not when he was like a Greek god, but when he had a strong, square nose like a cudgel, a boldly-blocked head like a helmet, and a jaw like a steel trap." [77]

Regardless of his strong and definite opinions about paintings, Chesterton for the most part declined to paint because he felt that it was beyond his talents. "There is nothing harder to learn than painting", he once wrote.[78] But still, he truly loved color, and he did a great amount of drawing with colored chalks. Some good reproductions of his color drawings can be found in his book *The Coloured Lands* and in Alzina Stone Dale's collection, *The Art of G. K. Chesterton.*

Looking here at a brief sampling from Chesterton's black and white sketches, we find for the most part that same playful undercurrent that is present in his writings. Recall from chapter 3 Chesterton's satiric poem about the artistic temperament spreading through society. The poem tells of an imaginative dream in which one by one the different classes of society decide to become self-consciously artistic. At one point it says:

> I had a rather funny dream
>   Intense, that is, and mystic;
> I dreamed that, with one leap and yell,
> The world became artistic.[79]

[76] *Common Man*, 115.
[77] *Defendant*, 117.
[78] *Autobiography*, 94.
[79] *Greybeards at Play*, 42.

The poem then speaks of merchants closing up their shops, followed by:

> And Cooks recorded frames of mind
> In sad and subtle chops.[80]

The satire here derives from Chesterton's belief that true artists are otherwise ordinary people who do art—and not some kind of hyper-aesthetic hybrids beyond the pale of the normal life.

Another satiric poem is called "Of the Dangers Attending Altruism on the High Seas". Here Chesterton poked fun at the overzealous humanitarians who do more harm than good

---

[80] Ibid., 44.

by seeking to help people who neither need nor want their help. The sailors have dragged a fish on board and have tried to give it all of the finest food and comforts that a *human* could want. When the gasping fish seems ungrateful, he is put on trial. At this point the poem goes:

> They seized him and court-martialled him,
> In some excess of spleen,
> For lack of social sympathy,
> (Victoria xii. 18).[81]

Here is G. K.'s accompanying sketch of the trial:[82]

Chesterton also dabbled in political cartoons, as can be seen in this pointed sketch from the cover of *G. K.'s Weekly*:

In this pre-World War II drawing, the Germans are shown kicking and hammering the cross into a swastika.[83] Here is Chesterton's clear comment on the Nazis' co-optation of the Christian church in Germany.

Finally, here is a Chesterton illustration found in Hilaire Belloc's novel *The Missing Masterpiece*.[84] The inscription on the drawing says: "Enthusiasm of Chelsea in the Presence of the Masterpiece".[85]

Again the satiric intent is obvious, as the thoroughly modern abstract is wildly acclaimed by the people of Chelsea. The joke not only pokes fun at abstract art, but it is also highly improbable that the common people of Chelsea would

[83] G. K. Chesterton, *G. K.'s Weekly* 18, no. 456 (December 7, 1933), cover.
[84] Hilaire Belloc, *The Missing Masterpiece* (London: Arrowsmith, 1929), 73.
[85] Ibid.

receive such a painting with wild enthusiasm. Here again, then, Chesterton returned to his theme that the true artist finds a way to communicate with the public.

There are many avenues for enjoying G. K. Chesterton. Here we have explored his various talents and have once again encountered his robust arguments on everything from the lies of historiography to the colors of cauliflower. It is well to end by reminding ourselves once more of the philosophical underpinnings upon which all of Chesterton's arts and opinions are grounded—the Christian view of humanity as the special creation in the image of the Maker of all things. It is to this essential theology of imagination that we now turn in the following chapter.

Chapter Five

God that Made Good Laughter

In Chesterton's novel *The Flying Inn*, there is a song called "The Song against Grocers", wherein he laments the displacement of communal dining in the public inns by the advent of grocery stores and private dining. The first stanza of this song runs like this:

> God made the wicked Grocer
> For a mystery and a sign,
> That men might shun the awful shops
> And go to inns to dine;
> Where the bacon's on the rafter
> And the wine is in the wood,
> And God that made good laughter
> Has seen that they are good.[1]

Laughter, joy, play, and frivolous nonsense were to Chesterton things very close to the core of the real Christian religion and the purpose of human life. He took it as an article of faith that God invented pleasure and that the forces opposing pleasure are in fact opposed to God. Even religion itself did not escape this opinion, as Chesterton considered too much seriousness to be a form of idolatry. In this regard he once wrote:

[1] *The Works of G. K. Chesterton* (Hertfordshire, Eng.: Wordsworth Editions, 1995), 148.

I do not like seriousness. I think it is irreligious. Or, if you prefer the phrase, it is the fashion of all false religions. The man who takes everything seriously is the man who makes an idol of everything: he bows down to wood and stone until his limbs are rooted as the roots of a tree or his head as fallen as the stone sunken by the roadside.[2]

Taking oneself and the things in one's life too seriously, said Chesterton, constitutes a false religion in which we forget the great commandment: You shall love the Lord your God with all your heart, with all your soul, and with all your mind.[3] In enjoying our God-given pleasures we are loving God; in letting other things destroy that enjoyment we are putting those things before God.

Chesterton went on to say that frivolity has a kind of holiness about it. In *All Things Considered*, he wrote:

It is not only possible to say a great deal in praise of play; it is really possible to say the highest things in praise of it. It might reasonably be maintained that the true object of all human life is play. Earth is a task garden; heaven is a playground. To be at last in such secure innocence that one can juggle with the universe and the stars, to be so good that one can treat everything as a joke—that may be, perhaps, the real end and final holiday of human souls. When we are really holy we may regard the universe as a lark ... that extreme degree of holiness which I have postulated as a necessary preliminary to such indulgence in the higher frivolity.[4]

This phrase "higher frivolity" was Chesterton's deliberate flying in the face of such important and somber endeavors as

[2] G. K. Chesterton, *The Uses of Diversity* (New York: Dodd, Mead and Company, 1921), 1.

[3] Mt 22:37.

[4] G. K. Chesterton, *All Things Considered* (London: Methuen and Company, 1915), 77.

"higher criticism" and "higher mathematics" and many of the other pretensions of higher education.

But the essential point to Chesterton was that God created joy and laughter, because they are in fact a very important aspect in the nature of God. A lengthy passage from *Orthodoxy* explains:

> Joy, which was the small publicity of the pagan, is the gigantic secret of the Christian. And as I close this chaotic volume I open again the strange small book from which Christianity came; and I am again haunted by a kind of confirmation. The tremendous figure which fills the Gospels towers in this respect, as in every other, above all the thinkers who ever thought themselves tall. His pathos was natural, almost casual. The Stoics, ancient and modern, were proud of concealing their tears. He never concealed His tears; He showed them plainly on His open face at any daily sight, such as the far sight of His native city.... He never restrained His anger. He flung furniture down the front steps of the Temple, and asked men how they expected to escape the damnation of Hell. Yet He restrained something.... There was some one thing that was too great for God to show us when He walked upon our earth; and I have sometimes fancied that it was His mirth.[5]

The giant secret of the Christian is the joy of God that natural reason cannot explain. One of the signs of a higher spirituality, said Chesterton, is the ability to let go of seriousness and give oneself to God's joy. "How sad that the word 'giddy' is used to imply wantonness or levity!" he wrote in *Alarms and Discursions*. "It should be a high compliment to a man's exalted spirituality and the imagination to say he is a little giddy."[6]

[5] G.K. Chesterton, *Orthodoxy*, in *The Collected Works of G.K. Chesterton*, vol. 1 (San Francisco: Ignatius Press, 1986), 365–66.

[6] G.K. Chesterton, *Alarms and Discursions* (London: Methuen and Company, 1927), 144.

Here is the source of Chesterton's aversion to that sour-faced judgmentalism that tries to pass for Christian piety. Here as well is Chesterton's pivotal connection between theology and imagination; it is in the God-given realms of joy and play and frivolity and nonsense that the imagination tends to find its most fruitful harvest. Conversely, the free imagination can be a great help in an appreciation of the things of the spirit. With regard to nonsense, wonder, and the spiritual, Chesterton wrote:

> And here we fancy that nonsense will, in a very unexpected way, come to the aid of the spiritual view of things. Religion has for centuries been trying to make men exult in the "wonders" of creation, but it has forgotten that a thing cannot be completely wonderful so long as it remains sensible. So long as we regard a tree as an obvious thing, naturally and reasonably created for a giraffe to eat, we cannot properly wonder at it. It is when we consider it as a prodigious wave of the living soil sprawling up to the skies that we take off our hats.... This is the side of things that tends most truly to spiritual wonder.... This simple sense of wonder at the shapes of things and at their exuberant independence of our intellectual standards and our trivial definitions, is the basis of spirituality as it is the basis of nonsense. Nonsense and faith (strange as the conjunction may seem) are the two supreme symbolic assertions of the truth that to draw out the soul of things with a syllogism is as impossible as to draw out Leviathan with a hook.[7]

There are echoes here of the Romantic objection to the Enlightenment's narrow view of humanity as a rational animal, as Chesterton asserts that it is impossible for reason to know the soul. But even more significant is his conjunction of nonsense and faith; a truly remarkable thought that questions

[7] G. K. Chesterton, *The Defendant* (London: J. M. Dent and Sons, 1907), 69–70.

the efforts of those whose apologetics seek to square Christian doctrine with human perception and reason.

Chesterton here rejected the Deism—what he called the "rational religionism of the eighteenth century" [8]—which claimed that nature and humanity are all part of a great mechanical clockwork set in motion by a disinterested Creator. He also rejected the popular scientism of his day, which saw humanity as the temporarily dominant animal in a great evolutionary struggle for survival. It was important for Chesterton to assert that faith rests, not on "a picture of the ordered beneficence of the Creation; but, on the contrary, a picture of the huge and undecipherable unreason of it". [9]

Consequently, the spiritual person is not the one whose imagination is restricted by the serious rationalism of scientism but the one whose heart is open to the joyful nonsense and unreason that lie behind those solemn categories and self-important distinctions. Chesterton's theology is an assertion that the Creator exists indeed; that this same Creator of the earth and the stars is the Creator of the bacon on the rafter and the wine in the wood; and that the God that made good laughter has pronounced them good. We are created in the very image of the God who created laughter, joy, play, nonsense, and imagination.

As our primal ancestors learned in the Garden of Eden, however, human joy always rests upon a condition. There is always something that must be done or not done, if we are to experience the pleasures that the Creator has in store for us. Chesterton always liked to point out that the children's fairy tales contain this profound theological truth. For example, he wrote:

> For the pleasure of pedantry I will call it the Doctrine of Conditional Joy ... according to elfin ethics all virtue is in

[8] Ibid., 69.
[9] Ibid., 69–70.

an "if." The note of the fairy utterance always is, "You may live in a palace of gold and sapphire, *if* you do not say the word 'cow' "; or "You may live happily with the King's daughter, *if* you do not show her an onion." The vision always hangs upon a veto. All the dizzy and colossal things conceded depend upon one small thing withheld.... In the fairy tale an incomprehensible happiness rests upon an incomprehensible condition. A box is opened, and all evils fly out. A word is forgotten, and cities perish. A lamp is lit, and love flies away.[10]

The Christian's mind of course goes to the Garden of Eden and a dozen other stories in the Bible where happiness hangs upon a condition. Chesterton's point is that as it is in fairyland, so it is on earth. The reason is that the writers of fairy tales have discovered an important law of real existence. Chesterton wrote:

Strike a glass, and it will not endure an instant; simply do not strike it, and it will endure a thousand years. Such, it seemed, was the joy of man, either in elfland or on earth; the happiness depended on *not doing something* which you could at any moment do and which, very often, it was not obvious why you should not do.[11]

Chesterton spoke of "the profound morality of fairy-tales; which, so far from being lawless, go to the root of all law",[12] and again of "the great mystical basis for all Commandments",[13] meaning that the Creator built conditional joy into the nature of existence.

The relationship between Romanticism and Christianity is important to understand, because there has been much in

[10] *Orthodoxy*, 258–59.
[11] Ibid., 260.
[12] *All Things Considered*, 191.
[13] Ibid.

literary Romanticism that is definitely incompatible with orthodox Christian doctrine. Yet here we have spoken of the works of Chesterton and other Christian writers as consistent with the Romantic reaction to the Enlightenment view of nature and humanity. The key here is that the Romantics were looking in the right direction but that their vision was still blurred—their Romanticism groped toward the truth, but only as if following the shadows on a wall.

Thus, the Romantic view of nature is correct insofar as it recognizes the reality that lies beyond human perception. The Romantic view of humanity is valid when it insists that the human being consists of much more than a highly intelligent animal. The Romantic propensity toward the mysterious, the strange, the wild and unpredictable is correct in that it at least allows the possibility of mysticism and deity. In this sense, then, Christianity can be seen as a focusing or fine-tuning of the broad Romantic world view. Or perhaps a better way of putting it is that the Romantics sensed the light of truth and groped in the darkness toward it, but in the historical fact of Jesus of Nazareth the light became clearly visible.

Regarding mysticism Chesterton had much to say, and again his concern turned toward the issue of sanity and madness. In *Orthodoxy* he said bluntly:

Mysticism keeps men sane. As long as you have mystery you have health; when you destroy mystery you create morbidity. The ordinary man has always been sane because the ordinary man has always been a mystic. He has permitted the twilight. He has always had one foot in earth and the other in fairyland. He has always left himself free to doubt his gods; but (unlike the agnostic of to-day) free also to believe in them.... The whole secret of mysticism is this: that man can understand everything by the help of what he does not understand. The morbid logician seeks to make everything lucid, and succeeds in making everything mysterious. The mystic

allows one thing to be mysterious, and everything else becomes lucid.[14]

The extant insanity of our day is firmly rooted in the widespread rejection of mysticism. The Romantics had sensed this
problem and had sought in their own way to correct it. The
Christian, of course, goes far beyond the generic mystic in
the realization that the Incarnation of the Christ was the
moment of intersection between temporal human history
and eternal mystical truth. To accept the mystery of Christ is
to see the world for the first time as it really is.

As joy, wonder, and mystery are essential to Chesterton's
theology, so is the notion of goodness. We live in an age
wherein "being good" tends to be thought of as something
appropriate for very little children or very boring people.
On the other hand, Chesterton sought to expose the lie that
the way to pleasure is through breaking the rules. In Chesterton's wonderful novel *Manalive*, a cynic declares that he
does not believe that being perfectly good in all respects would
make a person happy. To this popular truism one of the protagonists replies, "Well ... will you tell me one thing? Which
of us has ever tried it?" [15]

Again appealing to the fairy tales for his data, Chesterton
controverts the claim that stories of monsters and other threats
merely scare the children. On the contrary, they teach an
important lesson:

> Fairy tales, then, are not responsible for producing in chil-
> dren fear, or any of the shapes of fear; fairy tales do not give
> the child the idea of the evil or the ugly; that is in the child
> already, because it is in the world already. Fairy tales do not
> give the child his first idea of bogey. What fairy tales give the

[14] *Orthodoxy*, 230–31.
[15] G. K. Chesterton, *Manalive* (London: Thomas Nelson and Sons, 1915),
367.

child is his first idea of the possible defeat of bogey. The baby has known the dragon intimately since he had an imagination. What the fairy tale provides for him is a St. George to kill the dragon.[16]

The important lesson is that there is such a thing as good and that it is possible for the good to defeat even the greatest fears and evils. Chesterton explained further:

> Exactly what the fairy tale does is this: it accustoms him by a series of clear pictures to the idea that these limitless terrors have a limit, that these shapeless enemies have enemies, that these infinite enemies of man have enemies in the knights of God, that there is something in the universe more mystical than darkness, and stronger than strong fear.[17]

Here is an important linkage between early imagination and the concept of good overcoming fear and evil. Take away these early imaginative adventures, Chesterton said, and the result is a generation of bland agnostics having only relative ethics and an inordinate fear of everything mystical.

Ours is an age when a great many people cannot say with confidence that there is such a thing as objective good. The notion of good has been widely relegated to a cultural artifact—an arbitrary code invented by human beings in their attempts to forge society. However, Chesterton argues that there is indeed a positive good and that it originates in the Creator. "All other goods", he wrote, "are only manifestations of that supreme good, and must ultimately be referred to it".[18] Again, the pagan mystics sensed this good and groped toward it as best they could. In Christ the supreme good

---

[16] G. K. Chesterton, *Tremendous Trifles* (New York: Dodd, Mead and Company, 1910), 103.

[17] Ibid.

[18] G. K. Chesterton, *All Is Grist* (New York: Books for Libraries Press, 1967), 127.

became incarnate, and in Christian doctrine the definition of good came into focus.

In this view, then, good is not a relative term to be bandied about and ignored at will; it is more like a precious relic to be cherished and protected forever. Chesterton wrote in *Orthodoxy*:

> And my haunting instinct that somehow good was not merely a tool to be used, but a relic to be guarded, like the goods from Crusoe's ship—even that had been the wild whisper of something originally wise, for, according to Christianity, we were indeed survivors of a wreck, the crew of a golden ship that had gone down before the beginning of the world.[19]

That good is found in "the wild whisper of something originally wise" is Chesterton's way of saying that God created not only all things and all people but good itself. The fact that humanity has shipwrecked only means that we—like Robinson Crusoe—must value the good as a diminishing resource in a world bent on extinguishing its light.

Chesterton's theology was, of course, a direct challenge to the philosophy of materialism. In his *Autobiography*, he referred to the skeptical materialists as "crabbed, barren, servile and without any light of liberty or of hope".[20] Here Chesterton is not so interested in name-calling as he is in pointing out that there is something more—something wonderfully so much more—than what the materialists will allow themselves to believe. Speaking of the vast cosmos, for example, Chesterton wrote:

> Science boasts of the distance of its stars; of the terrific remoteness of the things of which it has to speak. But poetry

[19] *Orthodoxy*, 283.
[20] G. K. Chesterton, *Autobiography*, *The Collected Works of G. K. Chesterton*, vol. 16 (San Francisco: Ignatius Press, 1988), 170.

and religion always insist upon the proximity, the almost men-
acing closeness of the things with which they are concerned.
Always the Kingdom of Heaven is "at hand"; and Looking-
glass Land is only through the looking-glass.[21]

The point is not that the poet and the Christian can make these
things up but that there really is something more out there; and
the fact that there is more out there means that even the things
we see have a greater significance than first meets the eye.

"If things deceive us," wrote Chesterton, "it is by being more
real than they seem. As ends in themselves they always deceive
us; but as things tending to a greater end, they are even more
real than we think them." [22] How can things be even more real
than we think them? The answer, of course, depends greatly
upon what one means by "real". The materialist insists that only
what can be perceived is real. The mystic insists otherwise. The
Christian knows a reality beyond the pale of materialism, and
it is in fact this reality that gives everything whatever significance it has. The riches of a man become filthy rags. The greatest human wisdom becomes foolishness. The solid "realities"
wither like the grass. On the other hand, our neighbor in need
becomes Jesus himself.

In order to understand Chesterton's statement about things
"being more real than they seem", we need to know that
Chesterton viewed everyday life itself as a sacrament—as a
visible representation of important sacred events. In this view,
our daily decisions and actions represent an even more profound struggle between good and evil that is always raging
behind the scenes. This view is distinctly at odds with any
other-worldly mysticism that relegates the earthly present to
unimportance and with any world view like materialism that
relegates the mystical to nonexistence. In Chesterton's view,

[21] *Tremendous Trifles*, 233–39.
[22] G. K. Chesterton, *Saint Thomas Aquinas*, in *The Collected Works of G. K. Chesterton*, vol. 2 (San Francisco: Ignatius Press, 1986), 538–39.

both the material and the spiritual realms do indeed exist, but it is the spiritual that is in fact the more "real". The events of the material world are representations of the spiritual.

Given this understanding of Chesterton's sacramental view, we see that much of his commentary about the poetic and the mystical, and even about fairy tales, carries a great deal more theological meaning than we might at first assume. In his novel *The Ball and the Cross*, Chesterton's protagonist reflects that "all through his life he thought of the daylight world as a sort of divine debris, the broken remainder of his first vision."[23] It is among this divine debris that humanity can still find the joy, wonder, goodness, and mystery that comprise Chesterton's theology of imagination.

For the Christian artist, the challenge becomes how to find and communicate what is valuable in that divine debris. In *The Everlasting Man*, Chesterton spoke of "the sincerity of art as a symbol that expresses very real spiritualities under the surface of life".[24] The Christian imagination, then, lies on the far opposite end of the scale from the merely imaginary. As Chesterton so powerfully concluded:

> But imaginative does not mean imaginary. It does not follow that it is all what the moderns call subjective, when they mean false. Every true artist does feel, consciously or unconsciously, that he is touching transcendental truths; that his images are shadows of things seen through the veil. In other words, the natural mystic does know that there is something *there*; something behind the clouds or within the trees; but he believes that the pursuit of beauty is the way to find it; that imagination is a sort of incantation that can call it up.[25]

---

[23] G. K. Chesterton, *The Ball and the Cross*, in *The Collected Works of G. K. Chesterton*, vol. 6 (San Francisco: Ignatius Press, 1991), 401.

[24] G. K. Chesterton, *The Everlasting Man*, in *The Collected Works of G. K. Chesterton*, vol. 2 (San Francisco: Ignatius Press, 1986), 239.

[25] Ibid., 237.

Chapter Six

The Topsy-turvy Giant

Imagine a great, untidy hulk of a man, weighing well over three hundred pounds. Picture a large moustache and a careless shock of unruly gray-white hair escaping a precarious black hat. Add a grand cape and a walking-stick. Now fancy this amiable giant suddenly casting away his stick and throwing his hat into the air; hurling himself headlong into a handstand on the ground; and from thence attempting to catch his falling hat between his waving feet. Here is a fair picture of the man G. K. Chesterton. There is no evidence of the mature G. K. ever having done such a thing, but there is ample evidence that he would very often have done so if he had been physically able.

The inventor of such characters as Innocent Smith, Patrick Dalroy, and Gabriel Gale was an artist whose imagination frolicked through life like a giant doing cartwheels across the stage at some dignified and somber event. Chesterton was ever the controversialist, not because of some psychological propensity to opposition for its own sake, but because he so passionately opposed the extant ideas and forces that are inimical to our sense of wonder and gratitude. His many writings represent a lifelong campaign to frustrate the social world in its incessant attempts to stultify the human imagination.

Gilbert Chesterton was not raised on the fast lane to over-achievement. His childhood memories were of a leisurely and tolerant upbringing in which he and his younger brother were allowed to enjoy learning at their own chosen pace.

Yet by his fortieth year GKC was known throughout the English-speaking world as a brilliant journalist and illustrator, a great controversialist on the public debate circuit, an extremely popular essayist and writer of murder mysteries, a novelist, a biographer, a playwright, and a foremost apologist for the Christian faith.

"I am sorry", wrote Chesterton in his *Autobiography* regarding his upbringing,

> if the landscape or the people appear disappointingly respectable and even reasonable, and deficient in all those unpleasant qualities that make a biography really popular. I regret that I have no gloomy and savage father to offer to the public gaze as the true cause of all my tragic heritage; no pale-faced and partially poisoned mother whose suicidal instincts have cursed me with the temptations of the artistic temperament.[1]

Thus he begins the story of his life with a sarcastic disclaimer, lest any future biographer be tempted to psychologize about his parents and childhood.

There were, in fact, early childhood experiences that G. K. would remember for the rest of his life and that were undoubtedly influential in his imaginative bent as an adult. The most prominent is the toy theater that his father built for the pleasure of the brothers Gilbert and Cecil. Throughout his *Autobiography*, G. K. refers repeatedly to the tiny scene of a man with a golden key in his hand crossing a bridge to rescue a maiden in a castle. There were also the many childhood hours that Gilbert spent "drawing straggling and

[1] G. K. Chesterton, *Autobiography*, *The Collected Works of G. K. Chesterton*, vol. 16 (San Francisco: Ignatius Press, 1988), 38.

sprawling maps of fabulous countries, inhabited by men of incredible shapes and colours and bearing still more incredible names".[2]

As for religious training, there was little to speak of. Later in his life, G. K. would recall, "The general background of all my boyhood was agnostic",[3] in that even those religious instructors he had were for the most part men who did not really believe what they taught. By the time of early adolescence Gilbert had become largely a stamp from the mold around him—a philosophical materialist, an atheist, and a proponent of a vague sort of scientism and progressive evolution.

Chesterton's years as a schoolboy are an interesting study in purposes at odds. To all outward appearances he was a daydreamy, rather unmotivated student who seemed content to cruise along the bottom ranks of his class. He was an admitted failure in Greek and a disaster in Algebra, spending most of his classtime doodling cartoons or writing rhymes on bits of scratch paper. Eventually his unconventional behavior and verbosity won him two friendships that would endure for the rest of his life—one with Edward Clerihew Bentley and the other with Lucian Oldershaw.

With his friend Bentley, Gilbert developed his habit of making comic verse and expanded his hobby of spontaneous cartooning. Together the boys invented a fiction that the headmaster of the school was actually a mechanical dummy that the lesser masters would daily wind up and carry around to his appointed functions. This notion eventually became a serialized cartoon that Chesterton and Bentley secretly carried on over a period of months.

It was the influence of Lucian Oldershaw, however, that seduced this literary underground out into the open. The

[2] Ibid., 51.
[3] Ibid., 140.

son of an actor, Oldershaw possessed a broader view than did his two comrades. Though G. K. had been perfectly content in his anonymity and his secret artistic pleasures, Oldershaw convinced him to become a founding member of the Junior Debating Club. Soon the club was actually publishing its own journal, to which Gilbert contributed poetry and cartoons on a regular basis. In spite of G. K.'s reticence, the boys' talents were duly noticed by the schoolmasters, as Chesterton recalls:

> But, somehow or other, a rumour must have begun to circulate among the authorities that we were not such fools as we looked. One day, to my consternation, the High Master stopped me in the street and led me along, roaring in my deafened and bewildered ears that I had a literary faculty which might come to something if somebody could give it solidity.[4]

Soon thereafter, the astonished Chesterton found himself winning prizes for his poetry and earning the privileges of the top form in his school.

When his school days finally came to an end, Gilbert saw all of his friends go off to their various intellectual pursuits. "I said farewell to my friends", he reflects in his *Autobiography*, "when they went up to Oxford and Cambridge; while I, who was at that time almost wholly taken up with the idea of drawing pictures, went to an Art School and brought my boyhood to an end."[5]

At the Slade School of Art, G. K. Chesterton did not thrive. At the school he found that a few students worked enthusiastically at learning their craft, while the great majority merely "idled" and discussed nihilistic philosophy. G. K. recalls "that an art school can be a very idle place and that I was then a

[4] Ibid., 71.
[5] Ibid., 78.

very idle person".[6] It was during his time at the art school
that Chesterton experienced his period of "doubts and mor-
bidities and temptations";[7] a time when he discovered the
reality of evil and the lure of philosophical pessimism.

But then there came a remarkable moment when his mind
and imagination rebelled against the skeptical materialism
around him. In his *Autobiography*, he explains:

> When I had been for some time in these, the darkest depths
> of contemporary pessimism, I had a strong inward impulse
> to revolt; to dislodge this incubus or throw off this night-
> mare. But as I was still thinking the thing out by myself ...
> I invented a rudimentary and makeshift mystical theory of
> my own. It was substantially this; that even mere existence,
> reduced to its most primary limits, was extraordinary enough
> to be exciting. Anything was magnificent as compared with
> nothing. Even if the very daylight were a dream, it was a
> day-dream; it was not a nightmare.... Or, if it was a night-
> mare, it was an enjoyable nightmare. In fact, I had wandered
> to a position not very far from the phrase of my Puritan
> grandfather, when he said that he would thank God for his
> creation if he were a lost soul. I hung on to the remains of
> religion by one thin thread of thanks.[8]

Thus did young Gilbert Chesterton manage to dig his way
out of the sandpit of pessimism by finding that "mystical
minimum of gratitude"[9] that recognizes the miracle of mere
existence.

On the impetus of this newfound revolt "against the Deca-
dents and the Pessimists who ruled the culture of the age",[10]
Chesterton made his first moves toward a literary career.

[6] Ibid., 94.
[7] Ibid., 85.
[8] Ibid., 96–97.
[9] Ibid., 97.
[10] Ibid., 97.

He wrote poems emphasizing the folly of unthankfulness, and during this time he conceived the idea of Innocent Smith in the novel *Manalive*. When his father helped him to get a poetry collection called *The Wild Knight* published, G. K. Chesterton made his debut into the world of English letters.

The establishment of Chesterton's career as a journalist came almost incidentally during his time of languishing at the art school. Along with his friend Ernest Hodder Williams, Gilbert had been auditing some Latin and English lectures at University College. Knowing of Chesterton's connection with the art school, Williams gave G. K. some books on art to review for the *Bookman*, and a career was born. "I had discovered", Chesterton recalls, "the easiest of all professions; which I have pursued ever since." [11] To his dying day G. K. Chesterton insisted that he was primarily a journalist, who happened to dabble in the arts as well.

Realizing his own relative lack of talent and motivation in the visual arts, Chesterton left the art school to pursue journalism. Soon he began to attract literary attention with his poems, essays, and reviews. In the year 1900 his poems were published under the titles *Greybeards at Play* and *The Wild Knight and Other Poems*. In the years that followed, collections of his essays began to appear under titles like *The Defendant* and *Twelve Types*. During that decade alone he wrote nonfiction books on Robert Browning, Charles Dickens, George Bernard Shaw, and William Blake; five more collections of essays; four novels; a social commentary; and two apologetic works, including *Heretics*, and his masterpiece, *Orthodoxy*. During his lifetime, G. K. Chesterton would write more than ninety books and at least as many introductions to other authors' books.

[11] Ibid., 102.

But to return to our chronology of Chesterton as a young man, he soon began to discover that his vague sense of gratitude raised as many questions as it answered. This was the period in which he wrote *The Man Who Was Thursday*, a nightmarish novel of a man's search for meaning behind the madness. G. K. felt that there was goodness behind the madness of the world and that one ought not to be pessimistic but grateful. The issue rather quickly became: Grateful to what or whom?

At about this same time Chesterton began to speak at the various meetings of the "Societies" that were then the vogue in England. There he began to notice some remarkable facts. For one, there seemed to be an almost universal rejection of Christianity and yet an avid interest in other metaphysical issues. There seemed as well to be precious little discussion that one could call rational or even sensible. But the most surprising thing to Chesterton was that in the discussions there seemed to be one class of people who were invariably reasonable and obviously well informed—and those were the Christian clergy. Such a fact, of course, flew in the face of all the popular prejudices about "blind faith" and "ignorant servitude to dogmas".

One such clergyman was the Reverend Conrad Noel, a radical Anglican priest, who frequented such gatherings in order to keep in touch with the winds of popular thought. In attempting to recall where he first met Noel, GKC writes:

> I rather fancy it was at some strange club where somebody was lecturing on Nietzsche; and where the debaters (by a typical transition) passed from the gratifying thought that Nietzsche attacked Christianity to the natural inference that he was a True Christian. And I admired the common sense of a curate ... who got up and pointed out that Nietzsche would be even more opposed to True Christianity than to

False Christianity, supposing there were any True Christianity to oppose.[12]

It was this kind of clear thinking that caught Chesterton's attention and began to turn his thoughts toward the Church.

Obviously it was sometime between 1907 and 1908 that Chesterton's mind found its desired clarity, because in the former he wrote *The Man Who Was Thursday*, and in the latter he wrote his remarkable *Orthodoxy*. Only three years earlier, G. K. had written his *Heretics*, which criticized some of the major philosophies of the day. Upon reviewing that book, Mr. G. S. Street, an eminent critic, stated, "I will begin to worry about my philosophy when Mr. Chesterton has given us his."[13] Consequently, GKC accepted the challenge, and the resulting book, *Orthodoxy*, is one of the most remarkable pieces of Christian apologetics to be found anywhere.

Another pivotal friendship for Chesterton was that of Father John O'Connor, who served as the inspiration for the Father Brown mystery stories. Though O'Connor was very unlike the fictional Father Brown in physical appearance and demeanor, O'Connor's penetrating intellect and realistic knowledge of the depths and dimensions of evil gave Chesterton the seminal idea for the stories—the notion of a seemingly ordinary priest being able to solve the mysteries that others could not solve. Much to the author's surprise, the Father Brown stories proved to be so popular that G. K. Chesterton soon became a familiar name all over the world.

Though his upbringing had been agnostic, Chesterton pondered his way through a series of intellectual stages to a point where orthodox Christian doctrine became the only philos-

[12] Ibid., 152–53.
[13] G. K. Chesterton, *Orthodoxy*, in *The Collected Works of G. K. Chesterton*, vol. 1 (San Francisco: Ignatius Press, 1986), 211.

ophy that seemed to make sense. For GKC, nothing else seemed capable of dealing with all of the facts—especially the facts of humanity's highly unique endowments and of the reality of sin. All other philosophies, said Chesterton, denied either one or the other of these obvious facts and were therefore deficient as explanations of truth. Finally, having eliminated all other possibilities, Chesterton admitted that he was indeed a Christian, and he subsequently joined the Roman Catholic Church.

To understand the significance of Chesterton's life and works, it is necessary to look at least briefly at the historical times in which he lived and wrote. Born on May 29, 1874, Gilbert was truly a child of the Industrial Revolution, and his formative years were dominated by that hopeful scientism and commercial progressivism that so stirred Western Europe and North America during the last quarter of the nineteenth century. Amazing discoveries in science and technology were even then changing the dimensions and qualities of everyday life. During G. K.'s youth the industrial societies moved from horse-drawn carriages to automobiles and then airplanes, and similarly remarkable changes came in the fields of communications, medicine, and the physical sciences as well.

What is even more important, however, to an understanding of Chesterton is the ideological and ethical revolution that accompanied these material changes. For not only was this era a time of rapid scientific discovery, but it was a time when the great majority of the middle and upper classes of Western Europe and North America drifted away from their Christian traditions and espoused instead the new ideologies of scientism and progress.

As the nineteenth century waned, the perhaps understandable enthusiasm for the possibilities of science came to be transformed—through the works of popularizers like Thomas

Huxley and H. G. Wells—into a cultlike belief in science as the one and only arbiter of truth and falsehood. This cult of scientism rejected all things metaphysical or supernatural, and it held that mankind's only salvation lies in applying the methods of the natural sciences to all areas of life—including human behavior and ethics.

Furthermore, on the coattails of Charles Darwin's sudden popularity, the apostles of scientism were able to convince a great majority that all ideas and beliefs must stand or fall by virtue of their consistency with evolutionary theory. The widespread and unquestioned diffusion of this assumption is one of the more shocking phenomena in the history of European thought, as one marvels to see the experts in one field after another line up and attempt to square their theories with evolutionary "science". Even the liberal theologians—for example the Roman Catholic Teilhard de Chardin and the Protestant Albrecht Ritschl—came under the spell, each attempting to show how his conceptions of God would meet the standard of evolution.

Even among those who did not bother with thoughts of science and evolution, there grew a creed so compelling and so all-encompassing as to threaten to swallow all the rest—the creed of progress. The notion of progress served not only as descriptive of the technological marvels that were obviously taking place but as prescriptive of the direction in which the world was and ought to be heading. The mischief came when people began to consider any and every change to be progress. Then, as now, many came to welcome all change as necessarily good and to disparage all traditions as outmoded and bad. Such notions obviously ignore the very important data as to whether the given change is in fact beneficial or not. The heady locomotive of progress for progress' sake proved irresistible to a great many people at the turn of the century.

One of the fascinating things about G. K. Chesterton is how he began as a child of his times and ended as one of the world's most passionate and effective opponents to the most popular ideologies of his times. What occurred in Chesterton's life was largely a youthful acceptance of the whole enterprise of scientism and progress, followed by a painstaking series of intellectual questions and investigations, leading through stages of movement from materialism to idealism to supernaturalism to theism, and finally culminating in Christianity. It was really a process of elimination that brought Chesterton to Christian doctrine.

However, there is a consistency here that should not be overlooked. From his earliest fantasies at his father's toy theater to his mature conception of a theology of gratitude, Chesterton followed the thread of his imagination through the facts of his perception and the logic of his reasoning mind. In the end G. K. lays claim to clearer perception and purer logic than his opponents; yet at the same time it is his imagination, his sense of wonder, of miracle, of surprise, of play and laughter, that he says differentiates his thinking from theirs. In other words, to leave the imagination out of the picture of the human being is to settle for an incomplete and therefore inaccurate picture. No amount of precision in measurement or logical explanation can overcome incomplete or inaccurate data.

Thus, in the bigger picture, G. K. Chesterton's work can be seen as an important part of the Romantic reaction to the older Enlightenment views of humanity. In a certain sense, the controversies of H. G. Wells versus G. K. Chesterton are an echo of the earlier ones of Voltaire versus Rousseau. For it was Voltaire and his progeny who emphasized the rational human being as part of a great clockwork machine called Nature; and it was Rousseau and the Romantics who protested that humans are feeling and imagining beings as much

as they are rational. In the context of Victorian scientism
and progressivism, G. K. Chesterton again unfurled the ban-
ner of Romanticism and argued for the more complete picture of what it means to be human.

This very issue, in fact, is the major theme of Chesterton's
book *The Everlasting Man*. Here the author takes another look
at human history in a new light—or more accurately, in a
very old light newly illumined. For rather than accepting
the standard Enlightenment revision of human history, Chesterton recasts the flow of events into a Romantic perspective
that recognizes the essential facts of human beings as they
obviously are—a remarkable and unique aberration and prodigy in nature. Having accepted the fact of human unique-
ness, says Chesterton, one then sees that the Christian view
is the only one that gives a plausible explanation of human
history.

Here is why the arts figure so very prominently in Chesterton's arguments. Pointing out that we have found no records
of horses or monkeys having dabbled in even the most ru-
dimentary of artistic expression, Chesterton argues that the
arts show the difference between humans and other animals
to be qualitative, and not simply quantitative. The human
being is a different kind of creature, not simply more of a
certain kind of animal. This conclusion, of course, has tremendous implications with regard to evolutionary theory,
but here our interest follows the implications regarding the
arts. In Chesterton's view, the arts are the very essence of
humanity, the very thing that differentiates the human from
the nonhuman, in that sense the very breath of life from God.

By the time of his fortieth year, G. K. Chesterton was a
well-established figure in the world of English letters. Along
with his friend Hilaire Belloc, he became a famous spokes-
man for an economic order called distributism—grounded
in the doctrine that every man is entitled to a decent job and

a home of his own. Against his friend George Bernard Shaw he debated and argued endlessly, opposing Shaw's socialism and his faith in the Superman of the Enlightenment dream. Consistent with other Christian Romantics, such as Robert Browning, George MacDonald, and later C. S. Lewis, Chesterton used his writings—whether songs, poems, stories, or essays—to demonstrate the sense and validity of traditional Christian orthodoxy.

Gilbert Chesterton's story cannot be complete without mention of his beloved wife, Frances. At about age twenty-five Gilbert went along with his friend Lucian Oldershaw to visit a family named Blogg. There on a subsequent visit Gilbert met Frances, with whom he immediately fell in love. Later, in a letter to Frances, G. K. admits as much and repeats the remarkable thing he said to himself at his first sight of her:

> If I had anything to do with this girl I should go on my knees to her: if I spoke with her she would never deceive me: if I depended on her she would never deny me: if I loved her she would never play with me: if I trusted her she would never go back on me: if I remembered her she would never forget me.[14]

Due mostly to Gilbert's feeling of unworthiness for such a jewel as Frances, he was a long time in coming to the point of declaring his love to her. But when finally the moment of their engagement came, G. K. was beside himself with joy. In a letter to a friend he wrote:

Dear Mildred,

On rising this morning, I carefully washed my boots in hot water and blacked my face. Then assuming my coat with

---

[14] Maisie Ward, *Gilbert Keith Chesterton* (London: Sheed and Ward, 1944), 93–94.

graceful ease and with the tails in front, I descended to break-
fast, where I gaily poured the coffee on the sardines and put
my hat on the fire to boil. These activities will give you
some idea of my frame of mind.[15]

The letter then goes on to announce his engagement to
Frances and his hope that his friend will wish them well.

In 1901 Gilbert and Frances were married by his friend
Conrad Noel in the Kensington parish church. Throughout
their lives Frances was obviously fond of Gilbert, and to their
home she supplied the very virtues in which her husband
was so lacking. Frances managed the money, as G. K. had a
habit of giving it all away rather indiscriminately. She did
not try to make Gilbert over, but she did take care to make
him more presentable when he ventured out into the public.
There are many stories of G. K.'s absent-mindedness and pre-
dicaments from which his faithful Frances invariably bailed
him out. Most importantly, though, their hearts and minds
were moving in the same direction, and though both Gilbert and Frances came to their own decisions independently,
they were able to enjoy through their final years that rare
and priceless blessing of sharing the same faith.

After a lifetime of giving innumerable speeches and de-
bates, sketching perhaps thousands of pictures, and writing
hundreds of essays, scores of poems and stories, and about a
dozen novels, Chesterton finally finished writing his *Autobiography* in 1936. At age sixty-two he was still keeping up
the pace, but during the cold spring of that same year he
became seriously ill. A few weeks later he died, leaving behind his beloved Frances and no children.

The corpus of Chesterton's writings is so varied and delightful that many readers wonder where to begin their own
explorations of this remarkable Christian man. My own per-

[15] Ibid., 84.

sonal favorite is G. K.'s *Orthodoxy*, for its clear, profound, and lively defense of the Christian faith. Also his *Autobiography* is a sheer pleasure to read. Three novels come to mind: *Manalive*, my favorite for its celebration of the adventure and wonder for which we are created; *The Poet and the Lunatics*, for capturing Chesterton's unique thoughts on sanity and madness; and *The Napoleon of Notting Hill*, for its robust political symbolism. Some of Chesterton's most enjoyable essays are collected in *All Things Considered*, *All Is Grist*, and *Tremendous Trifles*. Of his few plays I like *The Surprise* best, for its clever comment on free will and obedience. Among Chesterton's poetry I like the playful rhymes best; most of these can be found in *The Works of G. K. Chesterton*, *The Collected Works of G. K. Chesterton*, vol. 10, and in *Greybeards at Play*.

Now having ventured together across the broad palette of G. K. Chesterton's imaginative works, we can understand more fully the rationale and reasons behind his passionate opinions concerning the arts. There has been much here to consider and enjoy, but there is very much more that we have not even mentioned. The Christian artist can benefit greatly from pursuing Chesterton's thoughts further, for here is a man whose faith and art were theologically inseparable. As a fountainhead of imagination himself, Chesterton personified his belief that Christian faith involves more than intellectual assent and moral conformity—that it very importantly includes our God-given capacity to wonder, to imagine, and to create.

BIBLIOGRAPHY

Aeschliman, Michael. *The Restitution of Man: C. S. Lewis and the Case against Scientism*. Grand Rapids, Mich.: W. B. Eerdmans' Pub. Co, 1983.

Chesterton, Gilbert Keith. *Alarms and Discursions*. London: Methuen and Company, 1927.

———. *All Is Grist*. New York: Books for Libraries Press, 1967.

———. *All I Survey*. New York: Books for Libraries Press, 1967.

———. *All Things Considered*. London: Methuen and Company, 1915.

———. *As I Was Saying*. New York: Books for Libraries Press, 1966.

———. *The Autobiography of G. K. Chesterton*. Vol. 16 of *The Collected Works of G. K. Chesterton*. San Francisco: Ignatius Press, 1988.

———. *The Ball and the Cross*. London: Wells Gardner, Dalton, and Company, 1910. Also in vol. 6 of *The Collected Works of G. K. Chesterton*. San Francisco: Ignatius Press, 1991.

———. *Basic Chesterton*. Springfield, Ill.: Templegate Publishers, 1984.

———. *The Club of Queer Trades.* In vol. 6 of *The Collected Works of G. K. Chesterton.* San Francisco: Ignatius Press, 1991.

———. *Collected Poetry.* Vol. 10, part I of *The Collected Works of G. K. Chesterton.* San Francisco: Ignatius Press, 1994.

———. *The Coloured Lands.* In vol. 14 of *The Collected Works of G. K. Chesterton.* San Francisco: Ignatius Press, 1993.

———. *Come to Think of It.* London: Methuen and Company, 1930.

———. *The Common Man.* New York: Sheed and Ward, 1950.

———. *The Complete Father Brown.* New York: Dodd, Mead and Company, 1951.

———. *The Defendant.* London: J. M. Dent and Sons, 1907.

———. *The Everlasting Man.* In vol. 2 of *The Collected Works of G. K. Chesterton.* San Francisco: Ignatius Press, 1986.

———. *Fancies versus Fads.* London: Methuen and Company, 1923.

———. *Father Brown Crime Stories.* New York: Avenal Books, 1990.

———. *Five Types.* New York: Books for Libraries Press, 1969.

———. *The Flying Inn.* London: Methuen and Company, 1919.

———. *Generally Speaking.* New York: Dodd, Mead and Company, 1929.

―――――. *The Glass Walking-Stick*. London: Methuen and Company, 1955.

―――――. *Greybeards at Play*. London: Elek, 1974.

―――――. *Heretics*. New York: John Lane Company, 1909. Also, in vol. 1 of *The Collected Works of G. K. Chesterton*. San Francisco: Ignatius Press, 1986.

―――――. *Lunacy and Letters*. New York: Sheed and Ward, 1958.

―――――. *Magic*. London: Martin Secker, 1913. Also, in vol. 11 of *The Collected Works of G. K. Chesterton*. San Francisco: Ignatius Press, 1989.

―――――. *Manalive*. London: Thomas Nelson and Sons, 1915.

―――――. *The Man Who Was Thursday*. In vol. 6 of *The Collected Works of G. K. Chesterton*. San Francisco: Ignatius Press, 1991.

―――――. *The Napoleon of Notting Hill*. In vol. 6 of *The Collected Works of G. K. Chesterton*. San Francisco: Ignatius Press, 1991.

―――――. *Orthodoxy*. In vol. 1 of *The Collected Works of G. K. Chesterton*. San Francisco: Ignatius Press, 1986.

―――――. *The Paradoxes of Mr. Pond*. New York: Dover, 1990.

―――――. *The Poet and the Lunatics*. London: Cassell and Company, 1929.

―――――. *Saint Thomas Aquinas*. In vol. 2 of *The Collected Works of G. K. Chesterton*. San Francisco: Ignatius Press, 1986.

―――――. *Sidelights on New London and Newer York*. London: Sheed and Ward, 1932.

―――――. *The Spice of Life*. Beaconsfield, Eng.: D. Finlayson, 1964.

———. *The Surprise*. New York: Sheed and Ward, 1953.

———. *Tremendous Trifles*. New York: Dodd, Mead and Company, 1910.

———. *The Uses of Diversity*. New York: Dodd, Mead and Company, 1921.

———. *Varied Types*. New York: Dodd, Mead and Company, 1903.

———. *What I Saw in America*. New York: Dodd, Mead and Company, 1922.

———. *Wine, Water and Song*. London: Methuen, 1915.

———. *The Works of G. K. Chesterton*. Hertfordshire, Eng.: Wordsworth Editions, 1995.

Dale, Alzina Stone. *The Art of G. K. Chesterton*. Chicago: Loyola University Press, 1985.

Peters, Thomas C. *Battling for the Modern Mind: A Beginner's Chesterton*. St. Louis: Concordia Pub. House, 1994.

Ward, Maisie. *Gilbert Keith Chesterton*. London: Sheed and Ward, 1944.

INDEX